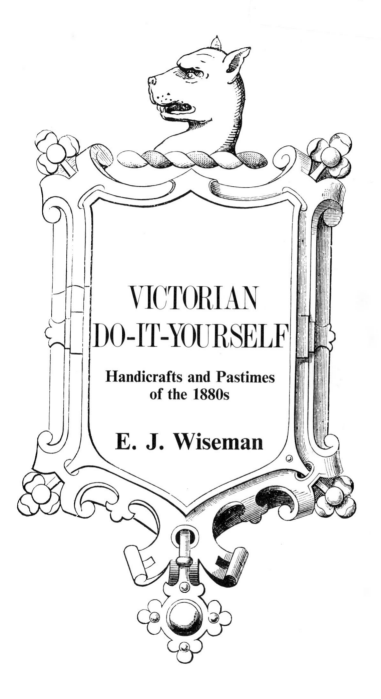

VICTORIAN DO-IT-YOURSELF

Handicrafts and Pastimes of the 1880s

E. J. Wiseman

David & Charles
Newton Abbot · London · North Pomfret (VT) · Vancouver

ISBN 0 7153 7307 2

© E. J. Wiseman 1976

Set in 11 on 13 pt Times
and printed in Great Britain
by Redwood Burn Limited Trowbridge & Esher
for David & Charles (Publishers) Limited
Brunel House Newton Abbot Devon

Published in the United States of America
by David & Charles Inc
North Pomfret Vermont 05053 USA

Published in Canada
by Douglas David & Charles Limited
1875 Welch Street North Vancouver BC

CONTENTS

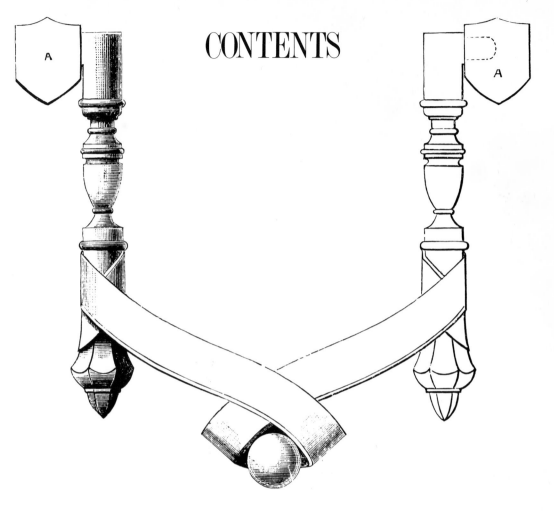

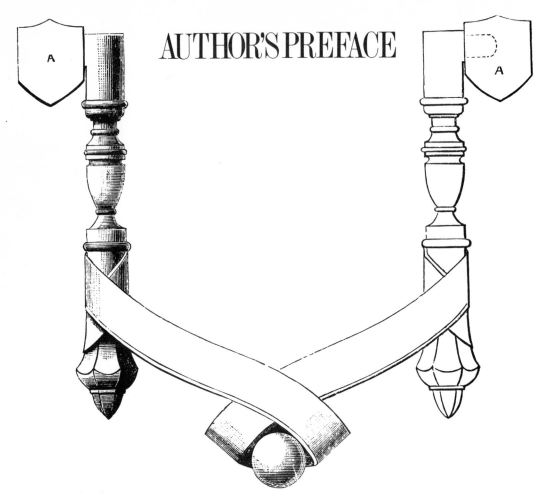

AUTHOR'S PREFACE

Amateur Work, Illustrated (1881–91) set out, month by month, in articles profusely illustrated by line drawings in the text and by folded supplements of working drawings, to show the Victorian paterfamilias how he might construct useful and decorative objects for the home. My own grandfather was a sub-scriber to this work for seven years and his half-leatherbound volumes have been available to me ever since I learned to read. Always fascinated by the magazines' contents, I think that their particular appeal today must lie in the fact that the material is addressed to the middle classes of that period. Although novelists have frequently given a picture of the very poor and of the aristocracy of the age, the detailed life of the middle classes has been less often described. To some extent, therefore, *Amateur Work* fills a gap in social history.

Merely to look through the yearly index of these volumes gives a striking picture of the sort of object which proved attractive to the Victorian home handyman. Few modern DIY enthusiasts would embark on the making of pipe organs, pianofortes, Elizabethan cabinets and iron fire-backs for fireplaces, much less velocipedes (bicycles) and the cumbersome photographic equipment of ninety years ago. Those of an electrical turn of mind were prepared to construct a winding machine to cover bare copper wire with layers of cotton or silk for insulating purposes, and had a plentiful supply of ideas for minimising the inconveniences of the messy wet batteries needed at that time for almost all electrical experiments.

Well seasoned hardwoods seem to have been readily available at a reasonable price, for the constructor is often told to use ¾in or 1in boards of oak, mahogany or walnut in widths which would be exorbitantly priced today, even if obtainable. Certain skills now gone out of fashion were quite common. It was taken for granted, for example, that almost any amateur would possess a woodworking lathe, and be able to use it. Fretwork was very popular and several ways of making one's own machine are described in these volumes. Facilities for having iron castings made from one's own patterns must have been widespread, for several instances occur in which the amateur craftsman is directed to make a pattern and to take it to a foundry to be cast. Wood carving was also commonly practised by amateurs, and much of the furniture described is intended to be ornamented in that way.

In his very lengthy introduction the Editor stresses that the contents are especially intended for 'the clerk, the curate, the struggling professional man and the man of letters' who may well be versed in the theory which lies behind various mechanical processes but stands in need of guidance in the practical details. Being intended for the educated classes, the magazine contributors assume that all readers can take Latin tags and French quotations in their stride, although they are not expected to see why a glass almost full of water will do duty as a makeshift spirit level (see 'Making a Tennis Court' in Chapter 3). Evidently a classical education was taken for granted, together with a complete ignorance of elementary science. I have quoted freely from the words of contributors, to illustrate their verbosity and love of classical allusion.

In Victorian times many magazine contributors were anonymous, the most painstaking searches by experts failing to identify those writers who sheltered behind noms-de-plume. The Editor also fails to identify himself by name, but admits that in his younger days he was an instructor in both woodwork and metalcraft in some kind of mechanics' institute in the north of England. His writings suggest that he was a man of little humour (possibly with a peptic ulcer) and given to considerable asperity when dealing with correspondents who did not heed his warning that he reserved the right 'of refusing a reply to any query that may be frivolous, or inappropriate, or devoid of general interest'.

The literary style of the Editor and his contributors is fascinating. It is obvious that we are dealing with a leisured society in which amateurs, anxious to receive help in their hobbies, are prepared to peruse papers containing 1,000 words of explanation as to why the contributor has written on his subject, or, not infrequently, a homily for or against the desirability of embarking on any particular construction. We are given a taste of this kind of thing even in the Editor's introduction.

That the present age is practical, and perhaps practical to a degree that has never yet been attained since the world was young, is to be attributed, on the part of some, to an unhealthy craving for money, as the means of acquiring luxuries of all kinds, and, on the part of others, to a healthy desire to utilise their time to the utmost, and to help themselves by doing many things for themselves for which, to a great extent, they have hitherto been almost, if not completely, dependent on others. Of these desires, the former degenerates into avarice or self-indulgence; but the latter blossoms into habits of thrift and manly independence and self-dependence.

The Editor brings his introduction to a conclusion by inviting experienced amateurs to submit articles—a suggestion to which they responded readily— and to make free use of the correspondence columns (a feature called Amateurs in Council). I have drawn freely on these letters, which will be found interspersed throughout the chapters, as they give a fascinating insight, not only into the minds of their writers and that of the Editor, but also cover a wide variety of popular Victorian topics and represent the views of a remarkable cross-section of society. For example, from the number of queries relating to the making of pipe organs one could conclude that these instruments were at that time as numerous as transistor radios are today! As the result of a 'Preliminary Notice' (put out by the publishers), even the first issue of the magazine contains letters from all over the British Isles—Putney (London); Thurso (Scotland); Plymouth (Devon); Cheadle (Cheshire); Dublin (Ireland), and one from Toronto (Canada). Very soon the magazine was attracting correspondence from France, Germany, India, Africa, Canada, Tasmania, the United States of America and even from St Helena and Ascension Island. Evidently *Amateur Work* met a real need.

Some queries reveal an astonishing ignorance of quite simple mechanical processes, while others show how readily the Victorian succumbed to advertisements with a scientific (or more usually a pseudo-scientific) flavour: eg 'electric' paint remover; 'magnetic' paint; 'Octopus' glue. Correspondents constantly pursue such will-o'-the-wisps as spring-driven vehicles and 'travelling per kite' in spite of sarcastic comments from the ever-vigilant Editor always on the look-out for 'the frivolous and inappropriate'.

No modern magazine could maintain its circulation for long if the editor adopted the same attitude towards his correspondents as the editor of *Amateur Work*—his abrupt admonitions would quickly ensure the early demise of any modern journal.

From the vast amount of material available to show the interests of the readers and the extraordinary attitude of the Editor towards those suspected of 'frivolity' I have selected the following:

Liquid Damp-proof Glue

J.B. (*Jubbulpore*) wishes for a good receipt for a liquid glue that will withstand damp during the monsoon weather in Eastern India when articles veneered or glued together give way and the veneering comes off. (Try the glue manufactured by the Gloy Company.—Ed.)

Ramrod fixed in Gun Barrel

SECOND ENGINEER was in the same fix as W.H.C. (*Wrotham*) but got out of it by unscrewing the nipple, putting in one drachm of powder, replacing the nipple, and firing the gun.—Ed.

Artificial Limbs

W.R. (*Kendal*). It would be useless to treat on the manufacture of artificial limbs because there is not one amateur in ten thousand who would take up the work in the first place or could carry it out successfully in the second.—Ed.

Elsewhere I have drawn attention to the reasons why so many clerics are to be found among the contributors. Craftsmanship had long been expected as an accomplishment of parsons, and in George Eliot's *Middlemarch* we find that 'Mr Brook suggested that Mr Casaubon [the Reverend Leonard Casaubon] should go fishing, and have a turning room, make toys, table-legs and that kind of thing.' Readers of *Middlemarch* will remember that Mr Casaubon was supposed to be suffering from mental exhaustion brought on by too much academic work. Now the novel was published in 1872 and this part of the story was set in 1831. Except that *Amateur Work* describes the making of fishing rods and flies, rather than their use, this could be a succinct synopsis of the magazines, for all the tasks mentioned by George Eliot are here explained in detail. But the Editor of *Amateur Work* would not have approved of George Eliot's way of life or her beliefs!

In making a selection from the great variety of crafts and objects described in these books, I have chosen items most closely associated with the home and garden, for these seem best to illustrate the way of life of the magazines' readers. It has proved difficult to condense so much sheer verbiage, contained in all seven volumes, into sections which give a general indication of an intricate lifestyle whilst, at the same time, describing hundreds of individual articles and their construction in detail. I can only hope that the reader will excuse any unnecessary brevity—the Victorians certainly would not have countenanced it —and will gain as much enjoyment and wonderment in exploring this book as I have from grandfather's old DIY manual.

INTRODUCTION

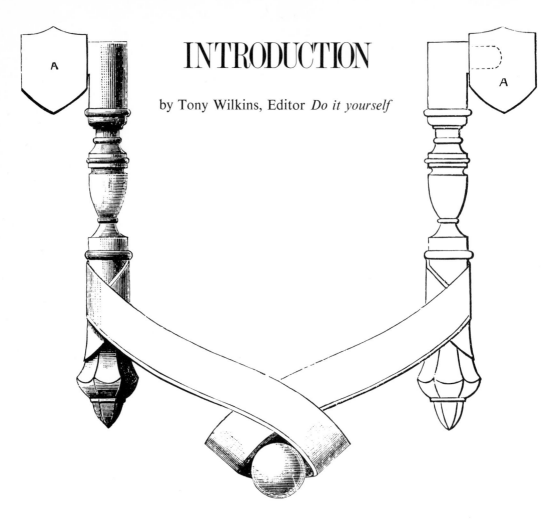

by Tony Wilkins, Editor *Do it yourself*

It is encouraging to be reminded that there is nothing new in the idea of 'doing it yourself'. Most of us come from families where only a few generations back folk lived by the skill of their hands. And I believe these skills, plus an inherent pleasure in handling natural materials lives on today. I'm sure our Victorian forbears with their love of verbosity would be horrified by such clipped phrases as DIY, and as you study this book you will realise that the projects they tackled were as far removed from ours in concept and design as the hot air balloon is from Concorde.

Theirs was an age of intricate heaviness. Ornate design laced with mouldings, carvings and fretwork. Where did they get the time for it all? I think the answer lies in the fact that it was the privileged man of leisure who made these things. He had help in the home, leaving him time to create. But his contemporary down the road, working long hours in factory or field, would have little time for DIY as the Victorians knew it. But through necessity he would be closely akin to us with regard to home repair and maintenance.

How I envy the Victorian man the time he seems to have had at his disposal. Time to doodle with the mechanics of a self-operating fountain; to build musical instruments or make a moving picture machine! And working with real things like wood, leather, iron, animal glue and glass. Ah, those were the days—for some.

The tools used would be those of the craftsman of the day, bought in the craftsman's own shops. Good and solid, heavy, but reliable like the materials they were designed to work. And there would be little feminine participation, I would guess, apart from the supply of tea and biscuits at the right time.

How the scene has changed over the years. Were our Victorian counterparts to come into a modern DIY shop there would be little that they could recognise A world of unknown plastics, packages and power equipment in gay colours— far removed from the traditional ironmongers with its rather dull surroundings and delightful range of smells.

After World War II, economic necessity started things moving. Everywhere looked drab after years of neglect; money was short, but there was a desire to start life afresh and to brighten the old place up. Returning craftsmen were, unfortunately, joined by amateurs setting up in business as painters and decorators—with little experience but lots of enthusiasm. And most householders soon realised that it was not difficult to equal, if not better the work they produced. There was a gradual awakening to the fact that the mystique surrounding many trades was merely a façade. Anyone willing to learn, practise a little and spend time on the job could produce a result of which they could be proud. The sacred preserve of the professional was being infiltrated!

At this time were born specialist DIY magazines, soon to have a combined readership of over ten millions. Magazines packed with ideas, hints, tips and gadgets; clear instructions in words and pictures on how to overcome such obstacles as rewiring the house, renewing the plumbing, building in brick, making furniture or drawing up your own plans. Feedback in the form of letters from readers highlighted the value of such publications, and it was soon clear that a new movement was underway. There was a great deal of satisfaction to be gained by doing things yourself, and there was pride in actually starting a project and seeing it right through to completion—in a way impossible in the conveyor belt factory world in which many now lived.

There was a growing awareness in industry that here was a vast new field where specialist products could be introduced to make jobs easier. Tools firms modified their designs and thought up new ones. Companies producing for the trade re-routed supplies in easily handled units and re-thought their marketing policies. From very small beginnings has grown an industry estimated to be worth, at the time of writing, in excess of £1,000 million!

The DIY boom affected all works of life—from the young couple setting up their first home on a limited budget, to the retired man with time on his hands and a little money in his pocket now able to create for the sheer enjoyment of it all. With the tightening economic situation, all families have become aware of the benefits of tackling jobs which are high on labour costs, until DIY in some form or other has become part of our way of life.

And it is not just the man of the house. Among the greatest enthusiasts and prime movers are the ladies. A deft hand with a paintbrush and an eye for colour make the whole thing a team effort—which has now moved into realms which would give our Victorian ladies the vapours even to contemplate. I have met women who have tackled the wiring in new self-built homes, dug drainage ditches, tiled roofs and put in rolled steel joists—and interest grows and grows.

With this growth came a host of new tools and materials. Ranges of amateur power tools and accessories, the invention of the paint roller, thin ceramic tiles which can be stuck in place, a whole new family of paints—one coats, thixo-tropics, water-based gloss—scores of new adhesives with immense strength, plastic products of all kinds. No solid timber for our modern handyman: man-made boards of wood chips covered in a veneer of timber or plastic. Pre-packed expertise with easy-to-follow instructions. Kits for wiring a house, fitting central heating, building a hi-fi system, a glass fibre boat, shelving, furniture—or a complete timber frame home with all the pieces ready numbered.

I don't think our Victorian handyman would be amused by the many short cuts we seem to take today. Ideas which take the craftsmanship away and replace it by engineering ingenuity. No more housed dovetail joints on drawers —but plastic sections which are merely cut to size and tapped together. No need for elaborate dowelling joints to hold components—but cunning little joining units which, at the turn of a screw, lock pieces firmly in place.

No more heating the old gluepot. Merely a squeeze from a minute tube to release a clear adhesive which sets on contact. And gone are all the beloved frills—though if you have a yen for the past, you can buy your mouldings by the metre, produced in plastic, ready to glue or pin in place. Pillars, alcoves, cornices and centrepieces all come ready moulded—together with rustic beams of foam plastic complete with wood splits and worm holes that can deceive the eye of the most experienced woodworker. Woodfinishing has been transformed too. No more the patient hours of French polishing. Instead the speedy, quick-drying plastic finish straight out of the can.

So the DIY movement continues to spread into fields undreamed of by the Victorians. The instant packaged garden swimpool, the solar heater to warm it, a room in the loft illuminated by a packaged dormer window, a home extension supplied as a kit. Many of these jobs call for tools used by the professional and not likely to be found in the handyman's outfit—hence the development of chains of hire shops. Once the province of the tradesman, their doors are now open to the DIY man who will be borrowing scaffold kits, cement mixers, power saws, woodworm killing kits, steam wallpaper strippers, specialist car tools, plumbing kits, damp-proofing kits, pneumatic drills . . . the list seems endless. Borrow for a day or a week—and instruction is given before you take it away.

All this may seem far removed from the leisure pursuits we read about in this book, but the wheel is turning full circle. Modern handymen and women have more time at their disposal, with flexible working hours in the office and four or five weeks' holiday. And so we are seeing a steadily growing interest in crafts and hobbies. Some old ones revived and some new ones using new techniques and materials. We can gauge interest by the figures of those attending evening classes and courses for further education—growing steadily every year—with, I believe, the women outnumbering the men. Do your own weaving, make candles, polish and finish semi-precious stones, make jewellery, cast in metal, tackle batik, woodcarving, pottery, enamelling—with or without a kiln, encapsulating picture framing . . . where will it all end?

It is hard to be sure, but with steadily increasing labour costs in every field of activity we can be sure that DIY is here to stay—on the one hand as a necessity and on the other for the pleasure it can bring. Maintenance will take on more importance. And this means your domestic appliances—as well as the one or two cars standing outside. We will exploit our gardens more for the food we need. We will try to harness the natural energy that surrounds us—and we will make far more use of the home and garden for leisure and entertainment as travel costs rise and the roads become more congested.

But before you feel spurred into action, sit back awhile and enjoy this fascinating book. Like me, I doubt whether you will be able to put it down until you've read it, cover to cover!

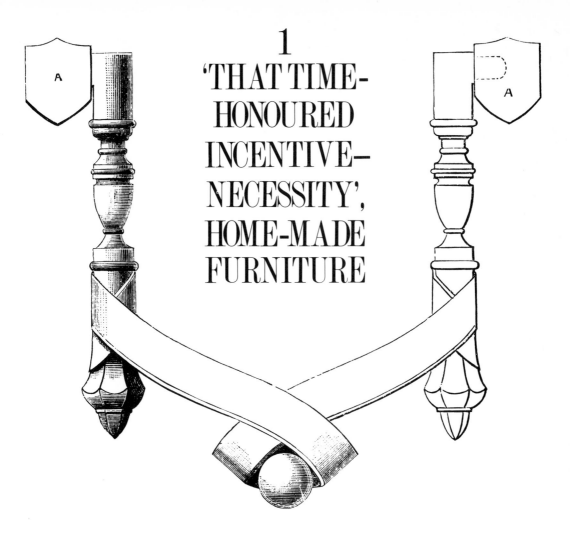

1
'THAT TIME-HONOURED INCENTIVE— NECESSITY', HOME-MADE FURNITURE

It is apparent, from the instructions given, that it is within the power of any bachelor who is possessed of a little ingenuity and assurance, to make the greater part of the furniture that is absolutely necessary for his rooms. What can be done by the unmarried man may be done by any one who has given, or is about to give, as Bacon terms it—'hostages to fortune'!

1 Armchair for sitting room or bedroom

2 Sidetable adapted to form a Canterbury (a cabinet for sheet music)

The late Victorians were optimists, looking forward to continuous progress and prosperity on the part of the white nations: more especially, of course, in the British Empire on which the sun never set and over which the old Queen‘ seemed destined to reign forever. This national outlook towards ever-increasing affluence perhaps explains the inclusion of articles in which thè complete furnishing of a house is described by one single contributor. He begins as a bachelor with simple needs and gradually elaborates his scheme to cater for a whole family, having explained to the reader that he hopes to get married soon.

Figs 1–6, taken from an early supplement, indicate the Victorian ideal of home comfort and convenience. The upholstered armchair (Fig 1) represents solid comfort, while the hanging shelves and cupboard (Fig 3) were much in demand by the housewife to display her numerous items of bric-à-brac. From the frequency with which designs for couches are given, it might appear that the Victorian female was still given to swooning, and perhaps we have cause to be grateful to today's emancipated women: certainly, the couch shown (Fig 5) would tax the ability of most modern DIY enthusiasts. Few nineteenth-century houses would be complete without a Canterbury (Fig 2), nor would one expect to see walls unoccupied by pictures, photographs or a small *étagère* (Fig 6)— a wall-bracket for displaying 'objects of artistic value', as one dictionary tells us.

Rather surprisingly, the number of fretwork designs included in the magazine is relatively small, though there are many references to new fretwork machines coming onto the market and even instructions for making one's own machine from items to be found in most homes and workshops. However, Fig 4 is a good example of the sort of thing the fretworker loved to make.

3 Hanging shelves and cupboard for bric-à-brac

4 Hanging cupboard in fretwork

5 Couch in imitation of Austrian bentwood furniture

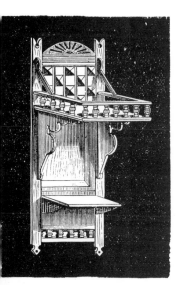

6 Small *étagère*: 'for objects of artistic value'

Furniture for Beginners

The young Victorian setting up a home for the first time thought in terms of solid utilitarian value. Even so, the contributor below claims some artistic value for his 'inferior' designs.

> I venture to say that the system of construction which I have to lay before [the reader], will be found the soul of simplicity. I can assure them that the articles so constructed will be strong; nor is there any reason why things thus made should not, in the hands of an amateur carpenter of good taste, become artistic.
>
> A few only of the most common tools will be necessary: a saw, a hammer, a gimlet, a bradawl or two, a chisel, and a screw-driver are all that are indispensable.

Strong and sturdy this simple furniture would certainly be, for the material recommended is mostly ¾in board.

Simple Table and Chair

The larger of the two tables (Figs 7 and 8) is 4ft 6in long, 2ft 6in broad and 2ft 4in high. It is suggested that the table top should be covered with American leathercloth (a material in common use up to the beginning of World War I) or with baize. The table's creator describes it as

> . . . decidedly ornamental, which is perhaps more than can be said for the Spanish washstand [Fig 9]. This latter article has, however, simplicity, quaintness and strength to recommend it. It stands firmly; it occupies the minimum of space and may be made in the length of a single winter evening.

7 Small occasional table of simple design

8 Large occasional table covered in American cloth

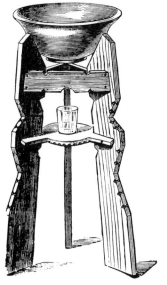

9 Spanish washstand for corner of bedroom

11 Bookcase: panels of cupboard ornamented with French wallpaper, embroidery, or pictures cut from illustrated papers

10 Chair of sturdy construction

The design of the side pieces in the chair (Fig 10) meant that 8in boards were needed which nowadays would be a costly item. Yet at that time the contributor advocated that such a model 'may well be made by the amateur for garden purposes'.

Simple Bookcase

The bookcase (Fig 11) is classed as an 'ambitious undertaking'. As the lower part had solid doors it was designed for use as an ordinary cupboard if required. The two parts were made separately for ease of movement.

The contributor suggests ornamenting the panels of the doors in the lower section by covering them with various materials such as 'a piece of French wallpaper, in imitation of embossed leather'.

Other materials may be used with good effect, as pieces of embroidery, brocaded silks, or even pieces of our now really artistic cretonnes: or a satisfactory use may be found for those large coloured prints, occasionally issued in the illustrated papers. Applied as panels and varnished over, they look exceedingly well; especially if a little brown pigment is added to the varnish, to tone down their too frequent garishness of colour.

The tendency to moralise seems to have been irresistible, even among lay contributors. In fact, some of these indulge themselves in this manner to a far greater extent than the many clerical writers. Continuing his series of articles at a later date, the previous contributor moralises still, giving an insight into his private life before passing on more constructional details.

It was not that I had any particular skill in carpentry, nor yet that I was hard up for occupation, that induced me to become the maker of my own furniture. ... Mine was that strong and time-honoured incentive—necessity ...

I could, of course, have hired or bought furniture, to be paid for in instalments, but such plans did not fall in with my views. I have ever held decided opinions as to the morality of running into debt. I was, moreover, proposing to marry as soon as I could do so with prudence.

He goes on to tell the reader that his 'daily occupation was of an artistic kind' which led him to make decorative features of such things as joints which could not be concealed, and 'boldly and openly to fix my work together with screws, using round-headed ones wherever possible, and making them also a decorative feature'.

Bedroom Furniture

Dressing-table

The design for a dressing-table (Fig 12) which follows, illustrates these ideas, as also do the towel-horse (Fig 13) and washstand (Fig 14). It appears that as his marriage draws nearer, he no longer is satisfied with his Spanish washstand!

The design for a bedroom chair (Fig 15) seems austere and the accompanying comments are rather mystifying. Why should his bedroom need four chairs?

Since we do not demand that our chair shall form a luxurious seat we do not propose to pad it—a cushion can be used if needed. ... At least a couple of these chairs will be required for the equipment of the bedroom, and, in some, perhaps, as many as three or four will be needed.

Although a wardrobe of the kind shown [Fig 16] is an article of very recent introduction [1885] there can be no question as to its great utility as a piece of bedroom furniture.

The suggested dimensions are 6ft 3in high, 4ft wide and 18in deep.

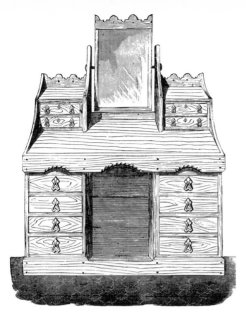

12 Dressing-table

13 Towel-horse

14 Pedestal washstand

15 Chair suitable for bedroom

16 Wardrobe with hanging space, shelves and drawers

17 Chest of drawers conveniently raised from the ground

18 Bedstead: part of the headboard of a bachelor's bedstead

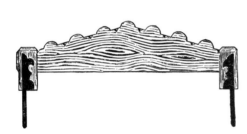

19 Bedstead: the footboard

20 Hallstand for hats, umbrellas and walking sticks

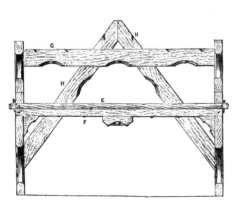

21 Hall seat or settle: front view

Chest of Drawers

He remarks that his own design for a chest of drawers (Fig 17) is unusual. It is higher in proportion to its width than the ordinary form and being raised from the floor is more convenient in use.

In the nineteenth century 'bedstead' was still a commoner term than 'bed'—the latter sometimes indicating the material on which one lay rather than the framework supporting it. Of the construction of his own bachelor's bedstead he writes that 'it will be found substantial enough to bear any bachelor of reasonable weight'. Fig 18 shows the bed head and Fig 19 the footboard. It was simply a 'trestle-bed' in which strong sacking was stretched between two side pieces joined to cross-legs at each end—undoubtedly a *bachelor's* bedstead.

Hints on the Utilisation of Waste Materials

The following reply from the Editor is an example of his heavy sarcasm handed out to those suspected of 'frivolity'.

> F.R.T. (*London*)—I am delighted to learn that you and your friends have found material in Amateur Work sufficiently funny to elicit 'roars of laughter' from you, individually and collectively. I have seen gum brushes of the kind described in many shops in London, and I have seen people looking at them, but the gum brushes, or rather the gum spreaders, have failed to excite their risible faculties. I hope you will not do yourself any serious injury by the paroxysms of laughter into which the information given by the contributor must inevitably throw you. Mr. R. Lewis, author of the article on waste materials is a practical engineer, who does not spell 'generally' with one 'l' as you do and as your friends probably do. You ask, 'Did Mr. Lewis invent these things, and does he through (*sic*) them away after using, or has he a heap of them at home?' I do not think he makes them to 'through' away, as it seems to you and your friends. I think he invented a good many of them but *Gardening Illustrated*, another 'comic' journal of a similar stamp to Amateur Work, was decidedly beforehand with him with the Cat-teasers, one of the applications which have made you 'larf'! I can assure you that the teasers are no laughing matter to the cats, whatever they may be to you and your congenial friends. You have never planted your slipperless feet on a hedgehog at the bottom of the stairs, I presume: if you did so and your friends were bringing up the rear, I fancy the bulk of the amusement would fall to their share, and that they would ejaculate, with Mr. Joseph Gargery, 'Wot larks!'—Ed.

In the Hallway

The contributor next pays attention to his entrance, 'by courtesy a hall, though more properly to be termed a passage'. The cumbersome outdoor clothing of the 1880s, together with the assortment of hats needed for a variety of occasions, occupied much space, so that with a drawer to house gloves, the hallstand (Fig 20) was an important piece of furniture. The contributor suggests a strong settle (Fig 21) to accommodate the kind of caller who would get no further into the house than the hall, but adds, somewhat sadly:

> . . . a time was at hand when a voice of greater authority than my own in household matters was to make itself heard in the house; and I was told that my settle looked cold and bare, and that something must be put in its place with more upholstery and colour about it. My business was only to obey. My settle was relegated to a distant part of the house, and, instead of it, I made two stools, one to stand on each side of my table [Fig 22].

22 Stool for use in hall   23 Bracket shelves for hall

Shelves and Cupboards

To complete the hall furnishing, the contributor made a set of bracket shelves, with cupboards (Fig 23).

The Snuggery

This same contributor, having dealt with the essentials for a bedroom and hall, omits all reference at this stage to the furnishing of a dining or drawing room. However, as we have already seen, he does look into the future, and realises that the time will come when he will seek privacy from his possibly increasing family. He thus proposes to appropriate a small sitting room, requiring little furniture, which he will eventually 'retain as my especial sanctum and snuggery'.

Octagonal Table

One essential piece of furniture was the octagonal table (Figs 24 and 25) which,

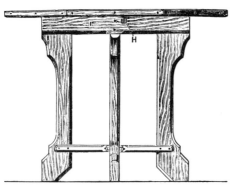

24 Octagonal table: front view

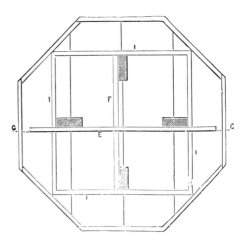

25 Octagonal table: plan

rather curiously, was to be covered with cloth secured by beading. Again American cloth is strongly recommended, but this would certainly not appeal to present day tastes.

He then outlines the other items to be constructed for his snuggery—a lounge chair, another chair for 'some favoured friend', a writing table, bookcases, for 'I am a reading man', and accommodation for antiquities, curiosities and several busts of which he admits he is a collector. The general impression is that the final result would be a completely cluttered up room such as we see in the illustrations of most interiors of that period. The set of bookshelves occupying a space 5ft 6in wide and 6ft 10in high is indicative of the dimensions of rooms of the 1880s which tended to be much higher and frequently larger than those found in present day homes.

The writing table (Fig 26) is of the same rather heavy design as all his other furniture, but at least appears functional. It is comparatively small, being 3ft 8in in length and a total height of 3ft 4in.

Glastonbury Chair

The armchair (Fig 27) is somewhat after the Glastonbury model, so-called after a type favoured by a former abbot of that place. The seat is of the normal wooden frame construction, with webbing and upholstery. The back is also of upholstered webbing and it is suggested that a little pad on each arm (not shown) should be covered like the seat and back.

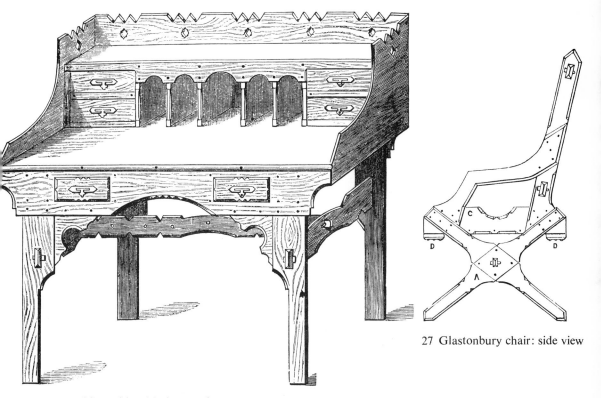

27 Glastonbury chair: side view

26 Writing table with dog-tooth ornament

I last made a small stand, or table [Fig 28], to set beside my lounging chair, where it would be handy to hold any trifling matter which I might wish to have near me, such as a book, a glass or a candle; and as I found it more especially useful as a depository for such appliances as I needed whilst indulging in the meditative pipe, I named it my Smoking Table!

Folding Lounge Chair

A 'Folding Lounge Chair', described in the July issue of 1887, is of interest, for while writing this chapter, correspondence developed in *The Daily Telegraph* regarding the invention of the common or seaside deck chair. A. S. W. Vaughan claims that 'the principle' of a folding chair, adjustable by means of notches, with a canvas back and seat, was pioneered by his great-grandfather, William Henry Vaughan, and his uncle, Samuel George Vaughan, and patented in 1880. Another correspondent claims that the first deck chair was made by Edward Atkins of Bethnal Green in 1879 and that the firm is still selling them at a much enhanced price! Finally Esmond Knight declares that he always understood that his grandfather Frank Barrett (real name Davis) was the inventor.

Whatever date is claimed, *Amateur Work* was abreast of the times for the contributor's chair (Fig 29) was in all respects identical with the modern article. Evidently it was not thought to be familiar to the majority of readers or there would not have been so many pictures of it—even details of fitting it together with washers and rivets seemed necessary.

Although he says his chair *would* do for garden use, the contributor has no doubt of its intended use indoors.

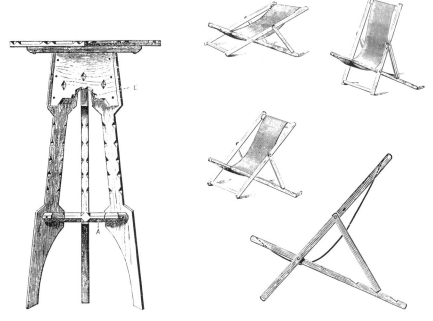

28 Smoking table for 'snuggery'   29 A folding lounge chair described in 1887, identical with our modern deckchair

Our chair finished, the last thing we can do is to sit down in it and enjoy the fruit of our labour, declaring it to be the most comfortable chair in the house for a tired and weary individual. As regards the *otium cum dignitate* of the matter, I think I am justified in asserting that no ease is so intimately associated with that phase of dignity which may be described as self-respect, as the ease which has been won conjointly by the exercise of brain power and the work of a man's hands.

Neo-Japanese Sideboard

Elsewhere in the magazine the same contributor describes a bachelor's sideboard 'in the neo-Japanese style' which so well illustrates the cluttered-up nature of furnishings of the period that it must be included here. The 1880s were the years in which there was a great revival of interest in all things oriental, and in particular a craze for objects bearing even a remote connection with the Land of the Rising Sun. The original drawing has been torn, but sufficient remains to show the design (Fig 30). Obviously the sideboard was a general factotum.

For a room that must need do duty as dining, drawing, smoking room, study and perhaps cellar, rolled into one, this sideboard boldly attempts to meet the demand by endeavouring to stand for sideboard, cabinet, bookcase, safe and cellaret, and throws in a few drawers and shelves in excess.

Oak or mahogany is suggested for its construction. I like the explanation of the term 'neo-Japanese': '. . . when anything is produced that cannot be immedi-

30 Neo-Japanese sideboard for a bachelor's dining room

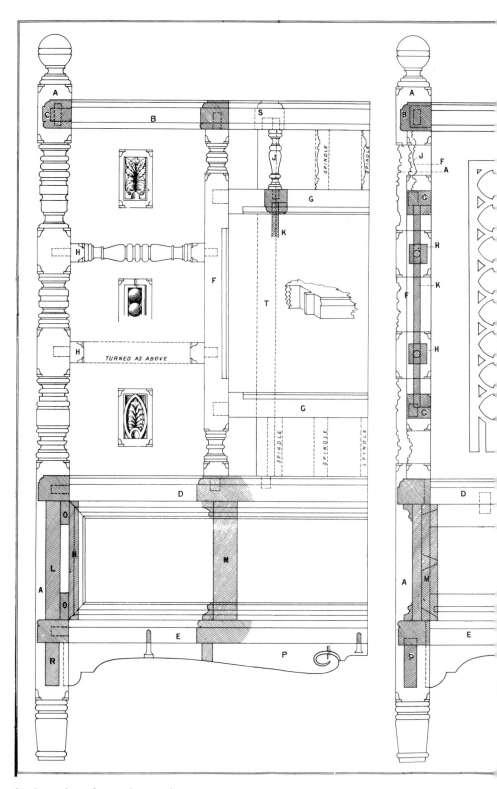

31 Canterbury for storing music

ately identified with any existing style, the term Japanese is always accepted as expressing it exactly'.

The Drawing Room

Music Canterbury

The music Canterbury (Fig 31) was an article for storing bound volumes of the more popular oratorios, where hard covers and gilt edges would rub shoulders with Mendelssohn's 'Songs without Words' and, perhaps, scores of the latest Savoy operas, while single copies of 'Come into the Garden, Maud', 'Excelsior' and other favourite Victorian ballads would occupy the drawer underneath. For a real sing-song, *The Scottish Students' Song-book* was always in great demand.

The origin of the name Canterbury for an article of furniture is obscure, for in the eighteenth century the term was applied to a fitted tray on a stand, intended for plates and cutlery, but Sheraton describes it as a container for sheet music, so called because such an article was first commissioned by an archbishop of Canterbury.

Our contributor devotes a column and a half to giving reasons why a piece of furniture 'not now so fashionable as it was a few years ago' still had a place in the home. The Canterbury could be wheeled to any part of the room. It need not stand against a wall like a cabinet. It could be placed close to the musician at the piano, or even, in the case of a grand piano, stored under it when not in use.

The Canterbury (Fig 31) is designed to offer scope for decoration by fretwork, turnery and veneering. As usual, the contributor concludes with a homily:

In this, as in all other matters worthy of attention, the injunctions of a well-known writer, who has been considerably quoted, may with advantage be remembered and acted on. You have very likely heard them before; as usually rendered into English his words are 'whatsoever thy hand findeth to do, do it with all *thy might*'.

The Kitchen

The final articles on simple furniture-making deal with items for the kitchen, notably a dresser and the ubiquitous corner cupboard. Dressers (Fig 32) are now more popular for display—only infrequently are they used as was originally intended, in the kitchen where they held all kinds of crockery on the shelves and cutlery in the drawers. These structures were wonderfully successful as collectors of dust on the china with which they were laden, but of course there were sufficient domestic staff available to deal adequately with this problem.

The making of corner cupboards was evidently quite compulsive, for few issues of *Amateur Work* omit instructions for such a piece of furniture in one form or another. Fig 33 shows such a cupboard, severe in pattern and utterly utilitarian in conception (in keeping with a kitchen into which visitors are unlikely to be allowed to penetrate).

The article on kitchen furniture brings us to the last few pages of our seven volumes to which this same contributor has supplied constructional articles on simple furniture over the whole period of seven years. The frequency of his papers suggests that he proved popular with the readers of the journal in spite of the long-winded introductions which preceded his practical details and his apparent inability to refrain from moralising on all possible occasions.

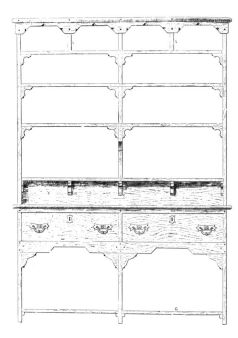

32 Simple dresser for kitchen

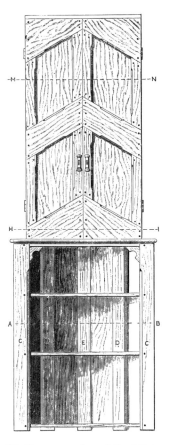

33 Corner cupboard for kitchen

2
'A TABLE WHATNOT FOR BRIC-À BRAC', DECORATIVE CARPENTRY

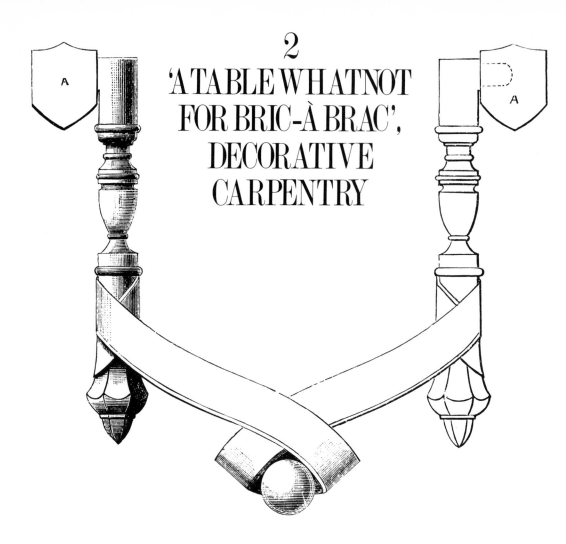

It is trying to the patience to put together a piece of mushrabiyeh work of some forty pieces, each of them so small that it is difficult to pick them up with the fingers; but the result repays the trouble.

'Decorative Carpentry for the artistic and useful adornment of the interior of every home' is the title of a series of *Amateur Work* articles on non-essential items apparently intended to assist the constructor in keeping up with the Joneses, not by a caravan or boat parked in the front garden, but by endeavouring to give a rather false air of grandeur to modest halls, dining rooms and parlours.

The Hallway

The hall in most Victorian middle-class houses was no spacious reception area but of 'modest width needing protection from the passage of people and packages'. Three suggestions for treating a panelled wainscot are given (Fig 34), the panels being filled with thin wood, tiles or pieces of the more costly kinds of wallpaper, old rolls of which could be bought cheaply at end-of-season sales. Out of the wainscot may grow (as it were) the design for the umbrella stand (Fig 35) requiring a hat and walking-stick rack above (Fig 36), for no self-respecting Victorian would be seen out of doors without both of these accessories.

34 Wainscot panelling for hall: three methods of treatment

35 Wainscot panelling with inserted umbrella stand

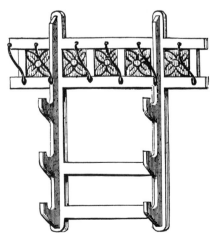

36 Hanging rack for hats and sticks

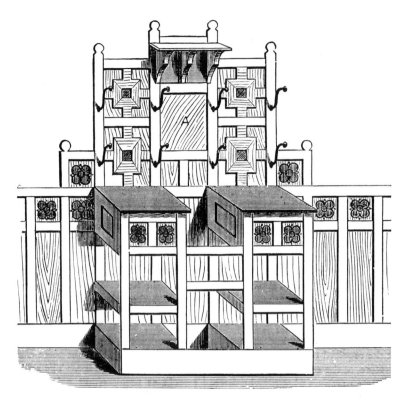

37 Hall table with hat and umbrella stand

Hall Table

A larger hall could accommodate a combined hat and umbrella stand with hall table and shelves (Fig 37). We are supplied with several modifications to coincide with the interests of the household. Immediately underneath the small tables could be drawers for gloves, while the lower shelves could be converted into cupboards to hold 'skates or other items not in daily request'. If skates needed to be stored so near the front door, it suggests that the impression which most of us have, that the weather pattern has changed over the years, is correct.

Corner Cupboard

Larger halls give an opportunity too for fitting in a corner cupboard. Very curiously, to my mind, the contributor suggests that such cupboards (Figs 38 and 39) should be repositories for more skates, tennis-bats (note *bats* not *racquets*) and the various accessories required for cricket, football and other sports, garden tools and gloves. He is evidently getting grander, for the shelves (Fig 39) are recommended to be used to hold a large pot or even a statue.

38 Corner cupboard and shelf for hall

39 Corner cupboard and shelf for hall: another design

Hall Screen

The screen (Fig 40) is recommended to enhance the appearance of a somewhat larger entrance hall and, before the advent of central heating, the drawing of the curtains helped to maintain the temperature of the dwelling. Once again shelves for bric-à-brac cannot be resisted.

40 Screen to divide up a larger hall

Overdoors

The contributor next turns his attention to a feature designed 'to give dignity and status to any room in which it is erected'. This is the 'overdoor'—a shelf above a door. It is not a nineteenth-century invention, for in various forms something of this kind is found in almost every age and not in England alone. The object in introducing an overdoor was to make a prominent and artistic feature of a necessary part of any room structure—the door or doors.

Pipes from Potatoes

LIGHT-KEEPER sends the following extracts from *Chambers's Journal* for January 1883: According to the *Vienna Agricultural Gazette*, it has been recently discovered that meerschaum pipes of excellent quality, susceptible to the highest polish, and even more readily colourable than the genuine *spiume di mare*, may be made from potatoes . . . [This was to be done by boiling the potatoes in dilute sulphuric acid for many hours.] The residuum of this simple process is a hard block of a delicate creamy white hue . . .

He adds: I forward the preceding, as I suppose it will be interesting to many of your readers, and I hope you will inform me how much sulphuric acid, and its price and postage, I am likely to require to make one or two trials. My boiler will be an old meat can, 6 inches deep, and 4 inches in diameter.

Fig 41 is a fairly simple affair decorated with plates under the main shelf. The shelf (Fig 42) uses ceramic tiles in decoration. The overdoor (Fig 43) has

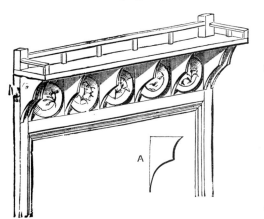

42 Overdoor with decorative tiles

41 Overdoor with shelf for ornaments

43 Overdoor with two shelves and covings decorated with Lincrusta

44 Overdoor: 'suitable for lofty hall'   45 Overdoor: 'in the Moorish style'

46 Overdoor incorporating a convex mirror   47 Overdoor with classical motif

covings of Lincrusta—a heavily embossed material much favoured for wainscots—under the shelves. One would almost believe that Fig 44 was especially designed to present the greatest hazard to those passing through the doorway, but it is strongly recommended by the contributor as 'a door in a hall . . . with plenty of space above, and in full view of passers-by up and down stairs'.

We are told that the advantage of an overdoor (Fig 45) 'in the Moorish style' lies in the fact that objects in the niches are somewhat protected from dust. Fig 46 makes use of a convex mirror while that in Fig 47 suggests a classical motif:

Those who aspire to reproducing this design, but have not the tools for working the fluted columns, may gain a similar effect by laying on thin strips of wood . . . glued and fixed with needle points; when painted, the effect is almost the same as square flutes cut in the wood, or half-rounded pieces may be placed side by side to give a reeded effect.

Fig 48 is intended as a prominent feature at the entrance to a library or drawing-room in the Gothic style. Note .the treatment of the door panels. Most of the decoration here is meant to be done in fretwork.

As the magazines progress, the overdoor designs become more flamboyant. Fig 49 is also meant for a library with bookshelves running all round the room. The Gothic overdoor (Fig 50) suggests the home of a church dignitary or successful lawyer. The shields could carry the arms of his family, his wife, his school, college and university.

Drawing Room

An example intended for a drawing room (Fig 51), shows the continued interest in oriental motifs—wallpaper and plates are chosen accordingly. The door

48 Overdoor: 'in the Gothic style'

49 Overdoor for a library

50 Overdoor: 'in the Gothic style, suitable for a dining room'

51 Overdoor: in the Anglo-Japanese style with matching panelling and wallpaper

itself has six panels achieved by removing all the mouldings round the original four panels (the normal number in a door) and inserting two transverse pieces mid-way between the upper and lower limits of the erstwhile upper panels which, of course, are usually twice as long as the bottom panels: thus six panels were easily obtained. The moulding on the jambs and lintel was hidden by a thin facing of wood to which decoration 'in the Anglo-Japanese style' was attached. The side panels were filled in with Japanese gold-lacquered paper readily obtainable in the 1880s.

Overmantels

Having reminded us that an important part of an Englishman's castle is his open fireplace

> in spite of all uncomfortable remarks from scientists, who say it gives the least possible heat for the greatest expenditure of fuel, and caustic remarks from the returned Cook's tourists and other cosmopolitans,

the contributor passes on to the decoration of fireplaces in parlours—a word he prefers to drawing rooms 'where nobody draws, or to which no one withdraws after dinner, except occasionally'.

Figs 52, 53, 54, 55 and 56 show designs for decorating several fireplaces, the last two showing Japanese influence, with a somewhat larger fireplace in Fig 57. We gain a fascinating view of an ordinary middle-class parlour in the latter part of the nineteenth century (Fig 58). Note the gasbrackets sprouting from the corners of the overmantel. The coal gas of those days being very imperfectly purified, the fumes produced by the products of combustion were a menace to plantlife and human beings alike.

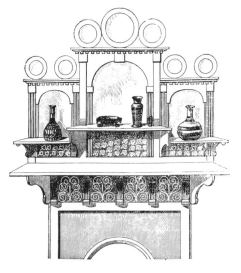

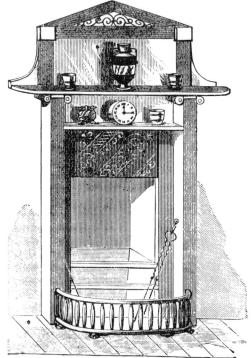

52 Overmantel of simple design

Right:
53 Overmantel for a small bedroom fireplace

55 Overmantel in the Japanese style

54 Overmantel added to an existing mantelpiece

57 Overmantel for a larger fireplace

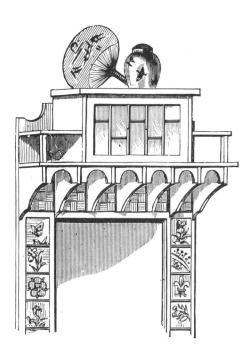

56 Overmantel including a glazed cupboard

58 Overmantel for a living room

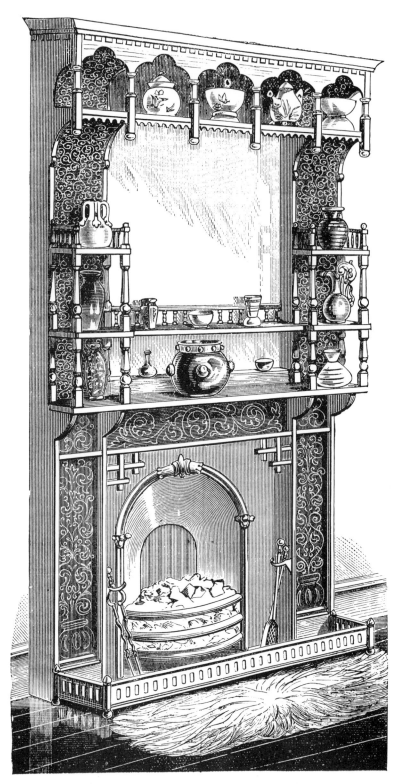

59 Drawing-room fireplace
before decoration

60 Drawing-room fireplace fitted with elaborate overmantel

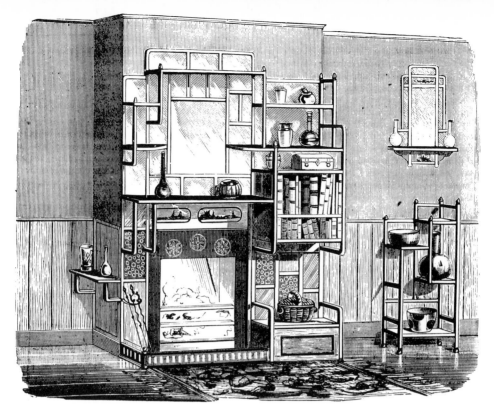

61 Fireplace decorated in the Anglo-Japanese style

Figs 59 and 60 are curiosities, showing the 'before and after' effect of embellishment on a modest design of fireplace: the combination of the Anglo-Japanese effect at the top of the fireplace itself, with turned pillars above, and 'Moorish' arches right at the top, is hardly a happy mixture of styles.

The Anglo-Japanese style is again apparent in the treatment of the off-centre fireplace in the projecting chimneybreast (Fig 61). As a companion piece we are given a design for an Anglo-Japanese firescreen (Fig 62) for which it is suggested that handpainted silk panels would be suitable.

62 Anglo-Japanese firescreen

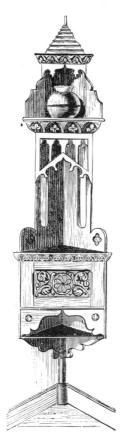

63 Corner cupboard showing oriental influence

65 Secretaire cupboards for a recess

64 Panelling and shelves for a smoking room or studio

The abhorrence of empty corners in a room seems odd to us—Fig 63 represents the typical Victorian obsession to fill up any corner that might otherwise present a naked appearance. Fig 64 is thought to be a most suitable decoration for a smoking room or studio while, oddly enough, the secretaire cupboards without the curtain (Fig 65) would almost fit in with modern ideas for functional furniture.

The contributor firmly believed in built-in cupboards and as a preliminary to a whole paper on such matters castigates his contemporaries for their dislike of them. We are therefore offered a bay-window seat with cupboards beneath (Fig 66) and a sideboard (Fig 67) recessed into a dining-room wall.

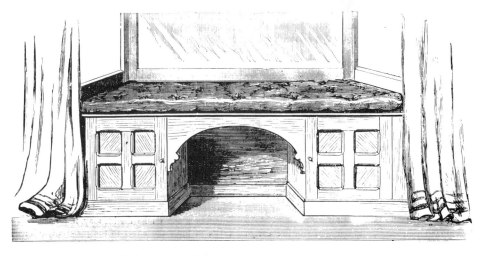

66 Seat and cupboards for a bay window

67 Sideboard for a recess

The recess in Fig 68 houses cupboards and shelves with a cove covered with Lincrusta or similar material. The merit of this construction is stated to be that the space usually to be found on either side of a pianoforte may be used as a bookcase and likewise, with more shelves above, the upper space is again not wasted. The cove above the pianoforte is not mere decorative detail, but is intended to have a beneficial acoustic effect, throwing the sound out into the room.

Gothic Couch

Lovers of all things Gothic might well have constructed this couch (Fig 69)— the decorative detail being an exercise in large-scale fretwork.

Whatnot

It would be difficult to improve on the following comprehensive definitions of two essentially Victorian objects:

> Fig 70 is a 'table whatnot for bric-à-brac'. It would be hard to find two words more vague in their meanings than these two. Whatnot, strictly though its use be limited to a certain series of shelves for the drawing room, shows that the word itself is as full of possibilities as the future; while bric-à-brac includes everything that one person throws away and another picks up and cherishes.

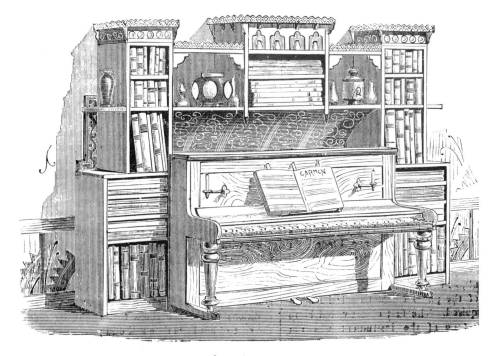

DETAIL
OF
CORNICE.

68 Utilisation of the space around an upright piano

69 Couch in the Gothic style

70 Table whatnot for bric-à-brac

71 'Alhambra' five o'clock tea-table

Whatnots, sometimes known as *étagères*, were frequently imported from the Far East, in sets to stand one upon another, to be free standing on the floor in one of those corners whose emptiness was anathema to Victorians. These *étagères* were sometimes built up to a height of seven or even eight feet in large rooms so that their instability must have been a constant menace to any housemaid responsible for dusting them.

'Alhambra' Tea-table

The 'Alhambra' five o'clock (how habits have changed) tea-table (Fig 71) is an exercise in fretwork for which full working-drawings are given in the magazine. Oiled straight-grained walnut was preferred, but as an alternative the structural parts could have been of black stained wood, the fretted areas being of satin wood or even gilded mahogany.

Jardinière

To describe the object in Fig 72 as a 'fancy jardinière' seems a monstrous understatement. The contributor lets himself go somewhat on a variety of subjects before getting down to the business of construction:

Flowers are unquestionably appreciated by the majority, and it is for lovers

46

72 Fancy jardinière

of these fragile but beautiful branches of nature that we pen our remarks.

Lovers of botany when among flowers are never without companions. A thorough knowledge of flowers is certainly useful in various ways and affords an acceptable subject of conversation, besides being of service to youthful couples wishing to correspond surreptitiously. Each flower has a special meaning . . . and conveys terms of endearment which are perhaps alone understood by the donor and recipient.

To the more cynical, the drawing may suggest the appearance of a novel liqueur stand for those who require a very plentiful and frequent 'stimulant'; but this suggestion must obviously be unfounded in these days of 'Blue-Ribbonism' and 'Good-Templarism'.

(Blue Ribbon wearers and Good Templars were members of popular temperance organisations which advocated complete teetotalism.) The structure again embodies much fretwork for which patterns were provided.

Screens

A contributor who had travelled much in the Orient became enraptured with the structures he saw there and adapted lattice designs to fit into various garden structures such as trellis doors and casements for summerhouses, and for

73 Examples of panelling in oriental lattice work

partial screening such as may be needed in restaurants. Fig 73 illustrates panels and borders of this kind. Fig 74 shows that much of this work can be done on the lathe while Fig 75 shows how the parts needed for the lower right-hand panel in Fig 73 are made up and put together.

Another contributor devotes two columns of the magazine (some 1,000 words) to explaining why screens are useful adjuncts to the 'modern' (1885) room, having been out of fashion for some time. They are recommended for breaking up a large room into 'snuggeries' (a favourite concept of the period) for various members of the family—writing areas, a corner in which the daughter could practise her piano and perhaps a special nook where the mistress of the house could keep her files of papers and accounts, newspapers and books. The writer concedes that a screen *might* even function as a draught excluder though he is a little shy of suggesting this, looking upon draughts merely as unsought-for ventilation to be encouraged in the same way as early-morning cold baths.

74 Detail of oriental panelling in the centre of Fig 73

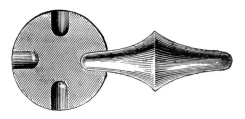

75 Wooden balls and conical pegs
used in another oriental panel

76 Folding screen decorated with scraps and prints

In the screens in Figs 76, 77 and 78 there is a suggestion of an over-all oriental design even though the details of most of the pictures are of western origin. The illustrations are fixed to calico or hessian tightly stretched over a wooden framework. Suggested sources for pictures include the covers of *Punch*, Pears soap advertisements and old prints from the original serialisation of Dickens's novels. Some screens should illustrate a theme—Shakespeare's characters, for example. A zoological screen was thought to appeal to children.

The screens in Fig 79 still show oriental influence while the *quatrefoils* at the top of Fig 80 and the heraldry of Fig 81 indicate an interest in medieval matters. Variety is seen in the curtain materials used in Figs 82 and 83. Fretwork and painting decorate Fig 84 while any watercolours produced by the family can be utilised as in Fig 85.

However, nowhere can we escape the *idée fixe* of all contributors—filling in a corner—in this case with a shelf 'that hooks the screen together, ensuring stability'. The purpose of the little side curtains escapes me.

77 Screen with floral motif

78 Screen decorated with cut-outs from magazines

79 Screen panels showing oriental influence

80 Screen with Gothic treatment
82 Screen using panel of curtain material
83 Screen incorporating matting in the panel

81 Screen with heraldic decoration

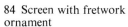

84 Screen with fretwork ornament

85 Screen for displaying the family's watercolours

86 Screen combined with table

Bracket Shelf

The bracket shelf (Fig 87) owes its origin to the Indian and Colonial Exhibition held in London in 1886 which seems to have inspired designs in the minds of several contributors. These shelves incorporate much fretwork in the top panels (Fig 88) and also in the main back panels (Fig 89) all of which would have been more easily done on a treadle machine rather than by hand.

Egyptian Coffee Table

A look at the elaborate Egyptian coffee table (Fig 90) will conclude this survey of oriental influences on design in the 1880s. It is an ambitious piece of work involving accurate joinery and much skill on the lathe. The main structure can

54

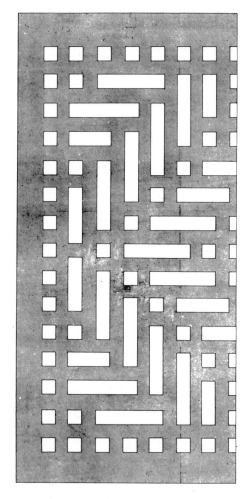

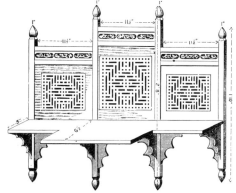

87 Bracket shelf 'in the Indian style'

88 Indian bracket shelf: panel design

89 Indian bracket shelf: design for decorative effects

90 Egyptian coffee table in mushrabiyeh work

be of beech or walnut while the star-shaped ornaments and small upright pillars should be light-coloured—perhaps in lemon wood. The contributor felt that the usual brass tray forming the top of such a table was too expensive, so that 'a top in keeping with Oriental style can be made of wood covered with Persian carpet'. The lattice work (called in Egypt 'mushrabiyeh work') must have taken the constructor many hours.

Fig 91, being a full-size drawing of one side panel, indicates how small many of the parts are, even though the side pieces marked A and B are turned all in one piece. In addition to eight pieces of mushrabiyeh work like Fig 91, forty pillars, as in Fig 92, and twelve drops, as in Fig 93, are required. The framework may be glued and pinned together, but with mushrabiyeh work this is never done—the various parts are merely held in place by pegging as shown. What DIY enthusiast would tackle such a job today?

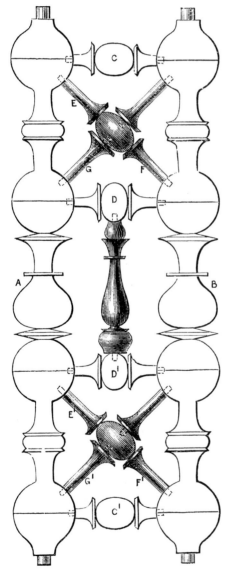

91 *Left:* Egyptian coffee table: turned work in side panels

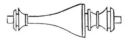

92 Egyptian table: turned spindle for mushrabiyeh work

93 Egyptian coffee table: drop or pendant for mushrabiyeh work

56

3
'AN ART FOR THE LITTLE SKILLED', RUSTIC CARPENTRY

Many frames of this kind cannot fail to catch the eye of the traveller in the gardens beneath him as he passes swiftly by the tops of houses by way of the district railways, through the suburbs of our larger towns.

The Garden

Having made the interior of his house 'snug', the Victorian handyman can turn his hand to improving his 'grounds'.

The Summerhouse

Perhaps Papa sees a small summerhouse where he can puff at his cigar without incurring the displeasure of Mama. Maybe our 'clerk, curate, struggling professional man and man of letters' has prospered and in his more spacious grounds can envisage a larger structure where the lady of the house can preside behind her silver teapot on summer afternoons when she is 'at home' to her friends. The days of grottoes and ruins were passing away, but rustic work was very much 'in', so that 'architecture in wood', as a contributor calls it, could be applied to many garden structures.

A series of articles on rustic carpentry begins with suggestions for three kinds of summerhouse. Figs 94 and 95 shows front and side elevations of such a building intended for a garden

> . . . of the most modest size. As an object of taste, a pretty summer-house, flanked by trees or evergreens, is pleasing to look at and by a little fore-thought may be made effective from the windows [of the residence]. I shall advocate a rough and ready mode of construction at which skilled carpenters may be inclined to sneer. Rustic work is pre-eminently an art for the little skilled.

Having encouraged the more timid craftsman with this last remark, directions follow regarding the best time to fell timber for building and suitable kinds to select. For a pleasing effect the bark is best left on; in which case it is best cut down in winter. If peeled work is preferred, the wood should be cut in spring when the sap is rising again. Because larch is second only to oak in respect of endurance, it should be our first choice of material. Examples of alternative woods are silver fir, common fir, spruce, ash and elm. Even apple wood, hazel rods, maple and wych-elm have their uses. The writer used apple wood for rustic seats and found it quite enduring.

Paint is, not surprisingly, condemned as a preservative for rustic construction, a coat of varnish or boiled linseed oil proving much more attractive.

After erecting the framework, the walls are next fixed in position. They are made of half-stuff (larch poles sawn in half, preferably by a 'steam-saw'—a sign of the times) as in Fig 96. The lining is, in its lower part, also of half-stuff, overlapping to exclude wind. Fig 94 shows clearly how ornamentation is introduced into the upper portion by using smaller half-stuff and arranging it in a diagonal pattern.

A finish to the four front posts is given by the addition of rustic capitals, formed by winding four sticks of large quartered wood round the pillars at the top, and four strips of smaller halved wood round the bottom of the cap, and fixing fir-cones between them with brads.

A 'summerhouse of medium size' is next illustrated (Fig 97). Rustic buildings

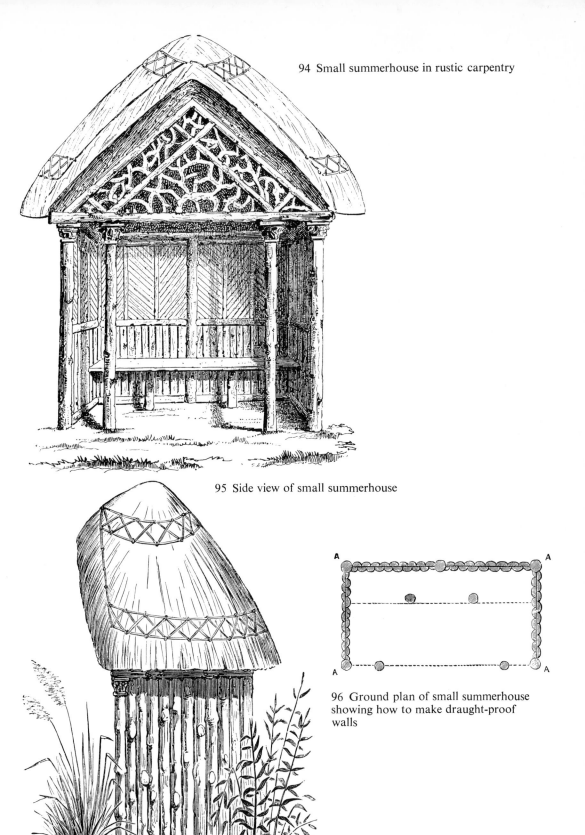

94 Small summerhouse in rustic carpentry

95 Side view of small summerhouse

96 Ground plan of small summerhouse showing how to make draught-proof walls

97 Medium size summerhouse

should, of course, be thatched—never tiled or slated. The writer advises that: 'A thatcher expects only the wages of a first-class labourer, and not those of a mechanic, and is not, therefore, a costly workman.' Ling or common heather is recommended for the lining of the roof.

If ling is not to be had, the ends of fir branches look very pretty. Perhaps a better substitute is furze. Failing any of these, a lining of moss will be found pretty, though not very enduring.

A much grander affair for the really big garden is shown in Fig 98—12ft long by 8ft deep with a height of 6ft. It carries elaborate decorative features including rustic mosaic panels (Fig 99) and a mosaic decoration for the seat (Fig 100) which looks very uncomfortable.

The floor area can be treated in two ways but 'a boarded floor is not suited to a rustic summer-house'. Pebbles (presumably washed and graded) will form a dry, sound and lasting floor, we are told, though 'ladies who wear thin shoes object to pebbles, as being hard and cold'. The second recommendation is to make a floor of lengths of round wood, driven into the ground vertically, very close together. The interstices are to be filled with sand.

98 Large summerhouse

100 Mosaic pattern for the seat of a summerhouse

99 Rustic mosaic panel for a summerhouse

102 Armchair in rustic carpentry

101 Small rustic table

103 Garden seat in rustic carpentry

Having eschewed planed wood completely, the contributor has difficulty in producing a flat surface for garden table tops, but surmounts the problem by building up a mosaic surface of very small rods (Fig 101). Small twisted branches of oak are technically known as 'bangles' and these are used in chair-making (Fig 102) where 'their crookedness may be used to good account'. A garden seat (Fig 103) uses oak for the main supports, the other parts being of straighter wood such as 'strong hazel sticks or small elm saplings'.

Amateur Dentistry

In reply to A PAPER STAINER a DENTIST writes: I believe in every man doing all he can for himself, or I would not regularly take in and read AMATEUR WORK. Get as exact a copy of the mouth as is possible. Do this by putting into the mouth a softened piece of beeswax. Any inaccuracy obtained by a faulty impressiol. will be found out when the work is completed. [!] Next, cast Plaster of Paris in the impression taken. Upon this fit the teeth. Place gold, platinum [then far cheaper than now] or dental alloy so as to fill up the required alteration: fix all the parts together with Plaster of Paris, put in borax as a flux and place a hard solder made according to the hardness of the metal. Apply a blowpipe and run all into one piece. Dress and polish.

COUNTRY BOD writes: I should like to write a short article on the subject. Dentistry is a subject with which amateurs should not meddle but oftentimes 'fools rush in where angels fear to tread'. I cannot insert any articles on dentistry in this Magazine—Ed.

Rustic Fences

Garden fences are dealt with in depth, being much in demand at that time especially in country districts where horses and other livestock were more likely to leave the road than even the most inebriated motorist. Fig 104, a light and simple fence of larch poles, is recommended as 'a safe protection against horses, cows and grown sheep; but'not against young pigs, lambs or poultry', whereas Fig 105 'will give full security'. The reader can see that the upper portion is proof against the larger livestock while, as the lower section has no opening more than 3in wide 'nothing beyond a very small chicken could find its way through'. Fig 106 is thought to be very pleasing to the eye but lacks the strength of the other models suggested.

Rustic Porch

The contributor thinks that 'few things add more either to the appearance or comfort of a cottage or small house than a porch' such as Fig 107. He believes that garden arches serve a purely utilitarian purpose as supports for climbing plants and therefore 'much elaborate design would be thrown away on them', though he concedes that Fig 108 would 'be picturesque from all points of view'.

  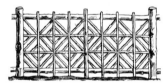

104 Rustic fence 'to keep out horses, cows and grown sheep'

105 Another fence: 'nothing beyond a very small chicken would find its way through'

106 Simpler fence: 'proof against most animals'

107 Rustic porch for cottage

108 Rustic arch for climbing plants

Step Stiles

Larger country gardens might have had a use for a step-stile. Fig 109 is designed for spanning a tolerably wide hedge and ditch while a narrow fence might be crossed by the more simple structure in Fig 110.

Sundials

A sundial in a wide expanse of lawn was thought to be both a pleasing ornament and of some slight practical use. The contributor believes stone pedestals to be quite appropriate in the formal garden but argues that a rustic pillar is not out of place in a rural setting. Fig 111 illustrates such a sundial with a quaint 'dogtooth' ornament made of fircones.

Stone carving is dismissed rather airily: 'There is nothing in working up a pedestal in free stone which need alarm any ingenious person', and a design is given for a combination dial (Fig 112) carrying dials on all four sides as well as on the top. Figs 113 and 114 are also suggested designs for dials.

The writer is lavish in his suggestions for suitable inscriptions for,

... the application of mottoes to dials is an ancient and praiseworthy practice. The Latin language has, on account of its terseness, been a favourite vehicle for these things. 'Noli confidere nocti' (Trust not to the night). 'Umbra sumus' (we are a shadow). 'Lex Dei lux diei' (The law of God is the light of day). 'Vigilate et orate' (Watch and pray). 'Pereunt et imputantur' (They pass away and are laid to our account). 'Ultimam time' (Fear the last hour). 'Fugit irreparabile tempus' (Irredeemable time flies away).

109 Step-stile to span a wide ditch or hedge

110 Step-stile to bridge a narrower gap

111 Rustic pedestal for a sundial

112 Combination sundial: a dial on each side as well as on the top

113 Design for ornamentation of an east-facing dial

114 Design for a horizontal dial

Recreation and Exercise

Garden Swing

Facilities for physical recreation were not neglected by contributors to the magazine.

> ... nothing can be more health-restoring or agreeable than outdoor recreation in the shape of gymnastic exercises, which are beneficial both to mind and body. Swings similar to that in Fig [115] enable one or two persons to swing him or themselves by the aid of ropes and handles attached to the ends of the cross-beams ... constant practice upon the swing is extremely useful, as being the only practical remedy against sea-sickness, the up and down motion of the swing resembling that of the ship on the water, it being a well-known fact that the gymnast, accustomed to the flying trapeze, feels no inconvenience in crossing the Channel, when his avocations call him to France, Germany or elsewhere on the Continent.

Giant Stride

The somewhat formidable looking apparatus illustrated in Fig 116

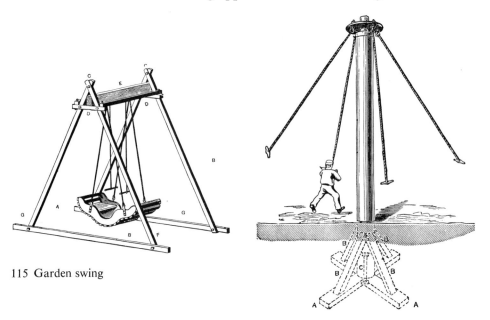

115 Garden swing

116 Giant stride: 'to promote health and vigour to the jaded frame of one too long employed in sedentary occupations'

> ... is in reality exceedingly simple in construction, while it affords at once healthy exercise, a continual fund of amusement, alike to youthful gymnasts and to men of mature growth. In fact no gymnasium can be considered

complete without its Giant Stride. In the gymnasia at the Crystal Palace and Alexandra Palace, and in other public gymnasia throughout the country, everyone must have observed stalwart men, flushed with the exercise, running and swinging round this aptly-named apparatus, with as much energy and vigour as though their very life depended upon the exercise, which indeed imparts so much health and vigour to the jaded frame of one too long employed in sedentary occupations that its popularity is as explicable as it is wide-spread.

If, as the result of this remarkable commendation, the amateur feels like making his own Giant Stride, he can cope with the wooden portions using a Norway spar or some other fir timber, but he will need professional help for some of the ironwork, though here again he may be able to make wooden patterns for a friendly foundryman to cast for him.

Lawn Gymnasium

Lapsing into the Latin which so frequently adorns the pages of *Amateur Work*, a contributor considers the Lawn Gymnasium (Fig 117) to be the *ne plus ultra* of gymnastic apparatus, as so many different appliances can be fitted to it. This

117 Lawn gymnasium convertible to a swing, a pair of hand rings, a trapeze, a horizontal bar and jumping stand

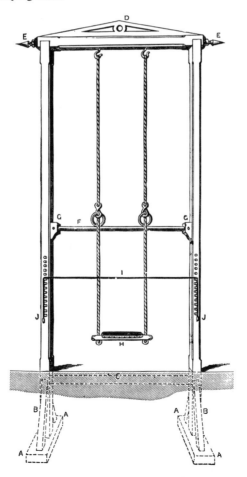

would make it particularly attractive to the Victorians who had a weakness for contrivances constructed to serve a multitude of purposes. This piece of apparatus could easily be converted from a plain sitting swing to a pair of hand rings, a horizontal bar, a trapeze or a jumping stand. If indeed this enthusiasm for gymnastics was as widespread as the contributor suggests, it may to some extent account for the colossal feats of endurance, despite their unsuitable clothes, performed by late Victorian explorers and mountaineers.

Horizontal Bars

Figs 118 and 119 are more or less self-explanatory illustrations of two designs for horizontal bars and here, in his final paper, the contributor really lets himself go in his eulogy of this piece of equipment.

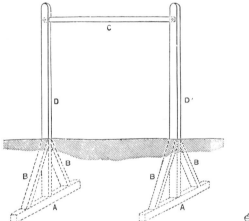

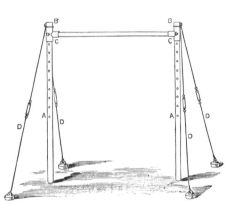

118 Wooden-framed horizontal bar   119 Horizontal bar with iron uprights

What the violin is to the orchestra, that the horizontal bar is to a gymnasium, and what the respectable fiddler is to the great violinist, that the ordinary performer on the horizontal bar is to the highly-trained and skilled gymnast . . . Occasionally gymnastic artistes make their appearance, as Avolo and others—whose performances entirely eclipse those of ordinary gymnasts . . . just as, in his day, Paganini, and in our own, Vieuxtemps and Joachim, astound their audiences, 'drawing houses with a single string'.

In 1874 Major Walter C. Wingfield patented 'a new and improved portable court for playing the ancient game of tennis'. This was the beginning of the modern form of tennis and led the All England Croquet Club at Wimbledon, finding itself in financial difficulties, to lay out grass tennis courts as an added attraction and add 'Lawn Tennis' to its title. The game is thought to have been introduced into the USA in 1874 by Miss Mary Outerbridge who had seen it played by Englishmen in Bermuda. Wimbledon Championships—among amateurs of course—were first held in 1877.

Lawn Tennis Court

It is therefore understandable that twelve years after the invention of lawn tennis the amateur worker is given directions for making his own tennis court. By that date grass, gravel, concrete and asphalt had been used for the purpose but a medical contributor describes how he made a court in his garden using tar and sand.

After emphasising the necessity for the complete removal of weeds from the site—by manual labour, of course, in those days before the introduction of herbicides—the contributor goes into the problem of levelling, suggesting at the same time that a slight fall towards the net, from both ends, will assist drainage if a small channel is made under it.

A spirit level was evidently not always readily available.

If a spirit level be not at hand a fairly accurate one may be extemporized with a glass of water almost full to the brim. When laid on a surface perfectly level, the water stands at the same distance from the top all round. If otherwise, the water approaches more nearly to the top at the part which is lowest.

It is surprising that the contributor thinks it necessary to explain *in such detail* the action of his homemade level.

Even with such common materials as tar and sand, the construction was somewhat daunting. One hundred and twenty gallons of gas tar were recommended and the tar had to be boiled before use. The amateur was advised to 'do this out of doors and not to wear his Sunday clothes'. The hot tar was to be poured on to the levelled surface, spread with a whitewash brush and immediately sprinkled with the sand.

Lawn-tennis Marker

With an interest in lawn tennis continually growing we find directions are given for a tennis marker (Figs 120 and 121). I particularly like the arrangement for closing the tap, without bending down, as an example of pure Victorian gadgetry.

The trough was made of a biscuit tin. Some of us can still remember the days when biscuits could be eaten without having to wrestle for ten minutes with an impenetrable plastic package, for then they were sold loose out of a tin box in which they were sent from the makers to the grocer. It is one such box which the contributor had in mind.

The tin was surrounded by a wooden case and into it was fitted 'an old wine or beer tap, which most people have with them'. This was purposely flattened somewhat at the mouth so as to spread out the jet of liquid whitening over the wheel. The wheel itself, of wood and covered round the rim with felt or flannel, was fitted on either side with discs of iron to keep the whitening from running

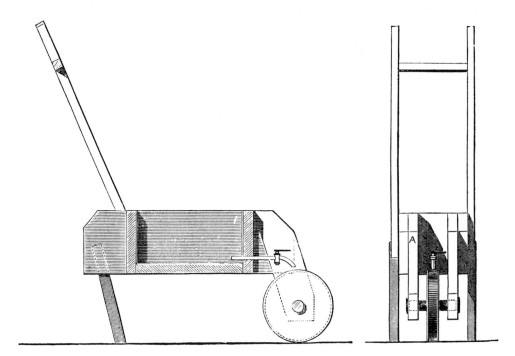

120 Lawn-tennis marker: side view

121 Lawn-tennis marker: front view

to waste down the side of it. The device for turning the tap on and off is described as follows:

> The only drawback was that one had to stoop down to turn the tap on and off, but this might be rectified by a strong spring made to keep the tap turned off, and a string brought round the outside and up the handle, running in wire loops, so that by pulling the string the tap was turned on and the spring turned it off immediately the string was slackened.

Tennis Racquet

Extraordinary pertinacity can only account for the introduction to an article on how to make a tennis racquet.

> It is not expected that the following instructions will enable anyone who has not seen a racquet to make one. These people are now few and far between. The writer's advice is, get one of the best made racquets to work from. [He means copy it as far as possible]. The ideas here are *the writer's own*, and were only perfected by him after two months' work in leisure hours, during which he failed *sixteen* times to steam and bend a bow successfully, though never doubting that success would crown his efforts, in which he was not disappointed.

> What could have been his motive in persisting so long? Did he wish to succeed merely for the pleasure he would get from achievement, or was he

70

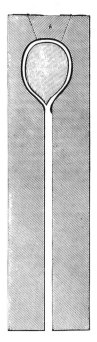

122 Lawn-tennis racquet: a homemade press, to operate round a template, used in bending a strip of ash into the shape of a racquet

trying to save money by making his own racquet? And why did the Editor accept a paper on a subject acknowledged to be very difficult? I would not myself have thought it worth all the trouble involved, even if the intention was to produce several racquets for a whole family, although the writer says that 'a steaming box, a template or block, and a press to force the wood round the template into the form of the racquet are all that are required'.

The scheme was that a template of 1in pine should be cut into the shape of the inside curve of another racquet. This was firmly screwed to the floor of the workshop. Then a gadget designed to force the material of the racquet round the template was contrived after the pattern of a gigantic nutcracker (Fig 122). The arms of this contrivance were about 5ft long and hinged to a cross-piece (A) by wrought-iron flaps. The cross-piece was also screwed to the floor. A long strip of ash was rendered fit for bending by heating the middle portion in a steaming box (a long wooden case plugged at each end by cotton rags) and into which steam was passed from a kitchen kettle for a period of one and a half hours. The steamed piece of ash was then quickly transferred to the template where the 'nutcracker' was applied to bend it into shape. It was secured by a clamp and left for a day to set. This was the process which needed sixteen attempts before success was achieved.

Having completed that portion of the work most fraught with hazards the contributor gives directions for incorporating a wedge (of walnut) in the centre of the racquet, finishing the handle and stringing. The article concludes on a note of triumph: 'From the foregoing details it will be seen that there is no difficulty which an amateur cannot surmount in making a racquet.'

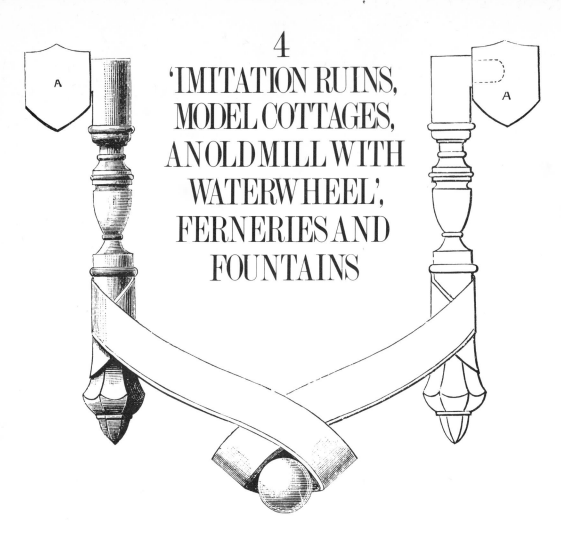

4
'IMITATION RUINS, MODEL COTTAGES, AN OLD MILL WITH WATERWHEEL', FERNERIES AND FOUNTAINS

Nothing is more interesting and attractive than a fountain, whether gushing out in a lavish display . . . in some public square . . . , playing gracefully in some quiet nook of a garden or whispering perfumed music in my lady's boudoir.

The floral displays in hotel and theatre foyers, in restaurants and gardenrooms may lead us to suppose that the indoor cultivation of plants, ornamental fishponds and trickling fountains is only contemporaneous with central heating and double-glazing, but our Victorian forebears forestalled us in the use of living material for internal decoration. Their scope was, of course, limited by the chillier conditions under which plants and creatures were expected to survive, but much pleasure was gained from rather attractive displays suited to the local environment in which it was often possible to establish a micro-climate conducive to the survival of the animals and vegetation.

Ferneries

Ferneries were extremely popular, for many species of these plants are capable of surviving in what must have been the rather arctic conditions of the Victorian parlour, away from the open coalfire and possibly subjected to icy blasts through ill-fitting windows.

Wardian Case Fernery

The easiest way to establish an equable climate was to use a Wardian case, a simple device used by Nathaniel Ward (1791–1868) a famous nineteenth-century plant collector, to transport plants safely from overseas to England. The case merely consisted of a sealed container with glass windows, so that while light could enter, the internal moisture could not escape, nor would the contents be subjected to too many fluctuations of temperature.

In the home, the Victorian fernery was essentially a Wardian case, but modified to be more ornamental in design. Such a case is depicted in Fig 123 —a simple affair of glass sheets standing on a zinc tray with a hipped roof, also of glass, all being fixed together by angled zinc strips and cement. A slightly smaller tray stands inside and is filled with a peat, loam and sand mixture in which ferns are planted. The space between the plant tray and the glass sides can be filled with fine shingle.

123 Rustic fernery

124 Open fernery with aquarium

125 Open fernery: foundation work   126 Open fernery, aquarium and fountain

Open Fernery

For live material which can stand fluctuations in room temperature, Fig 124 shows an open fernery surmounted by a type of aquarium which would be roundly condemned by present-day naturalists for it contravenes all accepted criteria as a satisfactory environment for fish. The foundation is made of zinc (Fig 125) and imitation rockwork contrived from coke chips and cement. As a teenager, I tried this myself and found that on weathering in the garden it finally gave quite a pleasing effect. The aquarium consists of what we used to call a propagating glass, being the forerunner of the modern gardener's cloche. They could be obtained in various sizes, but were all unsuitable for fish, for being taller than they were wide, oxygenation of the water was restricted and their round shape caused them to become unduly heated in a sunny window.

Fig 126 is another open fernery made even more attractive by a simple fountain worked from a small cistern hung on the wall above it and concealed by the curtains of the window recess in which the fernery stands. In this case a 'bee-glass' is chosen for the aquarium, in which case it will already be provided with a hole in the base for the entry of the fountain pipe.

74

Wall Fernery

Fig 127 shows how a dead wall can be converted into a fernery; the idea is indeed suitable for any modern gardenroom, though the contributor was thinking of utilising the wall on the shady side of small and crowded town-house gardens. The rough walls and plant pockets were made out of a mixture of coke and cement.

Fig 128 is intended for a 'handsomely furnished drawing room' and is therefore somewhat larger than those described above, being 2ft 6in long and of the same height. It is rather elaborately decorated and is intended to be painted in chocolate, white and gold.

127 Wall fernery

128 Fernery for a drawing room

Imitation Tree Fern

The monstrosity in Fig 129 is supposed to be an *imitation* tree fern. The stem or stump is made of a metal tube coated with cement scratched with a piece of wire, to imitate bark, just before it sets. In the stump are holes, out of which small plants may be made to grow. The stump is a rich dark brown, a colour much beloved of Victorians. It was placed in a large receptacle afterwards planted with lycopodium and small saxifrages. The tube of the stump was filled with suitable mould to maintain the growth of plants emerging from the stem and to support the 'luxuriant plume-like fern' planted at the top of the stump to give the effect of a tree fern. The contributor is sure this will prove an elegant table ornament.

Fig 130 is a combined fernery and aquarium containing a kind of rustic grotto to support ferns at the top and aquatic plants below. The rockery is once again of coke and cement on a framework made of soldered zinc bars.

The Oxford picture frame was a common Victorian ornament. Two of these are combined to form a fern case in Fig 131. The design at the base (to hide a

129 'Tree fern' contrived from cement and a 'luxuriant plume-like fern'

130 Fernery combined with an aquarium

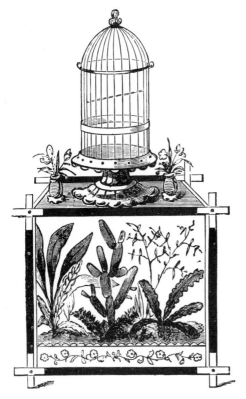

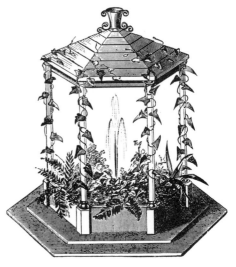

131 'Oxford' fernery with birdcage

132 Fernery in the form of a temple

zinc tray) is described as a 'paper imitation of embossed leather' attached to the glass.

Fig 132 is supposed to represent a rustic temple constructed on a hexagonal base using zinc tubes as pillars. The roof is really a tank filled with water through the funnel which surmounts it. Water descends through one of the pillars to the fountain and collects in the reservoir in the base.

Window-box Ferneries

Fig 133 shows a fernery projecting from a window of what appears to be quite an unpretentious house, while Figs 134 and 135 are evidently intended for a more affluent householder, if we may judge by the stonework around the

134 Windowbox fernery: another pattern

133 Windowbox fernery

135 *Right:* Windowbox fernery with bent glass front

windows. The heavy curtain rails of Fig 136 would be eagerly snapped up today as these items like much Victoriana are now very fashionable. The fountain in the case is to be worked in a simple fashion from a water supply coming from a tank on the wall (Fig 137).

Many Victorian houses were provided with bay windows—even a modest terrace dwelling was usually so equipped in its front parlour. Consequently we find our contributor giving designs for ferneries and fountains to fit into such windows.

Fig 138 depicts a design for a window in what appears to be a comfortably off home. It combines a shallow aquarium (a much improved feature) with a fountain and fernery. Two imitation tree ferns occupy the corners with hanging baskets on either side of the birdcage, which seems cruelly small for any live occupant. The fountain is operated quite simply by interchangeable tanks.

Just as some modern householders like to fill their gardens with gnomes, elves, storks and toads, so Victorians loved a 'ruin'. If rich enough, a ruined arch or broken tower could be contrived in one's garden, but the craze was not confined to the more wealthy: smaller ruins were admired in rockeries and ferneries. We therefore find that the contributor had received requests for guidance in constructing things of this kind. Although not providing illustrations, he tells us how such things can be made. 'Get a picture of some old ruined abbey, or such like, and endeavour to imitate it.' Thin slabs of cement were made on a foundation of coarse sacking laid on boards. These slabs were sawn up into small regular shapes and used (with the sacking marks outward) to form the walls of the 'ruin'. The amateur was told to break off pieces of the wall until the mode assumed the 'ruined' appearance desired. Windows and doors were cut out with a key-hole saw, the whole given a thin cement wash and tinted to taste.

136 Windowbox fernery with simple fountain

Far right:
137 Tank for supplying simple fountain

138 Bay window arranged to house a fernery, aquarium, fountain and birdcage

Any average amateur may successfully produce really good work in this way—besides imitation ruins, model cottages, an old mill with waterwheel, to work under trickling water, etc.

Mice Killing by Electricity

J.T.B. (*Malmsbury*) writes: Can anyone tell me if there is any arrangement for killing mice with a Leyden jar or otherwise? I saw a notice of such a thing in *Cassell's Family Magazine* some years ago. (Then why not hunt up the information required in the magazine in which you say you saw it?—Ed.)

Fernery and Fountain

Fig 139 is a design for a bay-window ornament combining an aquarium with a fernery. The foundation is a pillar made of zinc (a material easily soldered together) fixed to a metal base surrounded by a fretwork design also in zinc—this is to prevent the water from freshly watered plants dripping onto the carpet. The rustic rock work covering the base and stand is again of coke and cement, the pillar being filled with broken coke or stones for greater stability. 'The

139 Pedestal fernery with aquarium

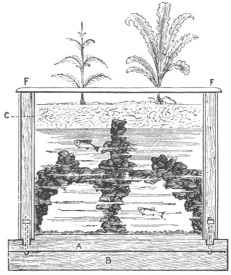

141 Large aquarium: end view

140 *Below:* Large aquarium with water plants and fernery

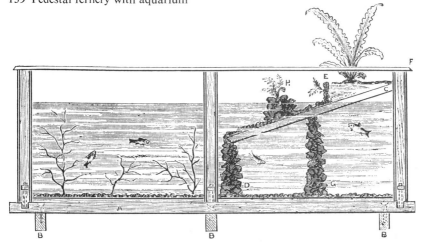

stand looks very handsome and massive if painted and varnished black, with the points picked out in bronze and gold.'

From the centre of the octagonal aquarium rises a 'ruin' on a four-arched framework and surmounted by a plaster figure (a female bearing an urn) 'which may be obtained at most image shops for about 1s 6d' (7½p).

Aquaria, etc

Fig 140 and Fig 141 show side and end views of a freshwater aquarium of a design which suited the taste of Victorians, being rather 'fussy' and incorporating the inevitable 'ruin'—used in this case to create a 'cave' for timid fishes and to support a 'beach' on which plants could grow. Some perfectly sound advice on fish-keeping follows constructional details, and plants suggested for the rockery include seven varieties of *Asplenium*, *Polypoides* and the *Equisetum sylvaticum*. As oxygenators below water level, *Vallisneria* and Quillwort are recommended.

Vivarium

The imposing 'building' (Fig 142) was originally designed in 1858 as a home for

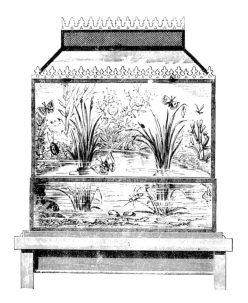

142 Vivarium combined with an aquarium

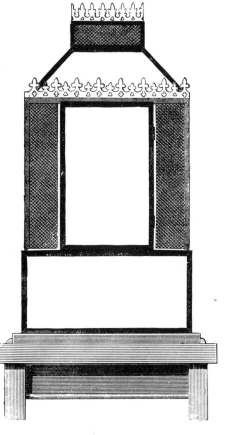

143 Vivarium: side view showing zinc gauze for ventilation

butterflies, but appears to be a vivarium more suited to aquatic insects. The lower section is, in fact, an aquarium extending from the glass front in the form of a curve across to the left-hand back, thus leaving space for 'land' on the right and back of the case. The side view (Fig 143) shows the glass door for access to the interior and the perforated zinc walls for ventilation. The 'land' portion of the interior was filled with earth into which were plunged zinc tubes concealing bottles of water, for the stalks of the plants required by the insects. No further details for stocking the vivarium were given, for the potential constructor was referred to the book by H. Noel Humphreys *The Butterfly Vivarium or Insect Home* from which the contributor had taken the design and adapted it to his own purposes.

Fountains

> Nothing is more interesting and attractive than a fountain, whether gushing out in a lavish display of water in some public square . . . , playing gracefully in some quiet nook of a garden or whispering perfumed music in my lady's boudoir.

So runs the introduction to a series on the making of fountains where, after a digression to show how the simplest fountain can be made to work by the force of gravity alone, as seen in the garden fountain in Fig 144, the contributor concentrates on the construction of 'self-acting' fountains, that is, a fountain in which the water supply is lower than the level of its basin, the water being forced up into a jet by air pressure. This also meant that the fountain was self-contained, portable, and suited to indoor use.

144 Garden fountain worked from a hillside lake

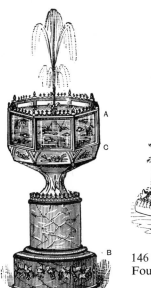

145 Patent Auto-pneumatic Fountain to play for five hours

146 Rushton's Self-acting Fountain

147 Self-acting fountain designed by a contributor

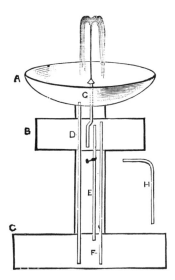

148 Rushton's Fountain: internal construction

Self-acting Fountains

The general appearance of 'self-acting' fountains is conveyed by Figs 145, 146 and 147. Fig 145 is a commercial model, made in two sizes. The smaller would play for five to six hours while the larger model performed for up to eight hours, depending on the number of holes in the jet. As all three fountains work on the same principle it is worth while taking some note of their ornamentation before considering their mode of operation. The opulent appearance of an imitation marble plinth was meant to appeal to the Victorian purchaser who would also be attracted by the ivyleaf decoration of the base and, I suspect, the finicky fencing round the plinth and aquarium top. Fig 146 was invented by J. H. Rushton of Horncastle and was on sale 'for the small sum of 15s 6d [77½p]'. We are not told its size, but it could play for forty minutes and be started again in half a minute. Again, its decoration is rather fussy and appears to incorporate two of the imitation tree ferns beloved of another contributor. As it was capable of being copied by an amateur, a diagram of its internal construction was given, Fig 148.

To operate the fountain, water is poured into the basin A, whence it flows into tank C via the pipe D, leaving the basin half-full. Tap E is closed. The bent pipe H is then attached to the top of D and air blown in, forcing the water out of tank C up into tank B. Tank C is now empty and tank B full. On opening the tap E, water from the basin A falls into C driving air from it up pipe E into tank B, thus forcing the water in tank B to rise through the jet G— the fountain plays. When it finishes playing, E is closed once more and pipe H used again to re-start the fountain.

The fountain (Fig 147) was designed by the contributor who, he tells us, 'sold scores of them ten years ago'. It is decorated in chocolate and gold paint. The machine was modest in design (being only 2ft 6in high) and in performance, for it operated only for an hour. The whole was constructed out of sheet zinc and 'compo' pipe—the sort of material once in common use for water pipes. Fig 149 shows a section of the fountain, its modus operandi being somewhat like those above, except that a pump is used to introduce air to the lower tank and no taps are needed in the pipes.

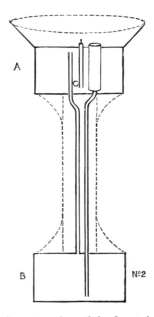

149 Internal construction of the fountain in Fig 147

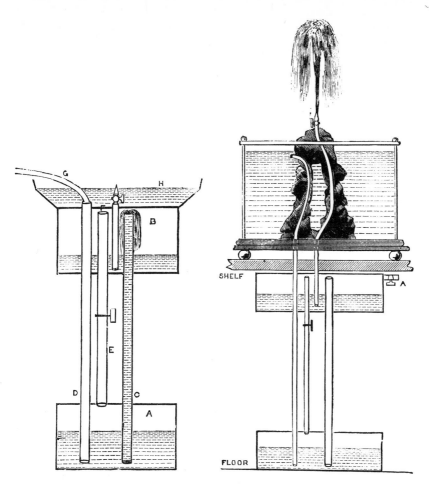

150 Another arrangement of pipes for a self-acting fountain

151 Self-acting fountain above an aquarium

The wide tube on the right, protruding into the basin from tank A is the barrel of the pump, made by rolling sheet zinc round a broom handle and soldering it. The contributor points out that brass is useless 'since the galvanic action between the brass and zinc would soon destroy the work'. The piston for this pump is also made from zinc using an umbrella ring as a sealing device and not forgetting to include a simple valve in the plunger.

To operate the fountain, water is poured into the basin until no more will run down to the bottom tank via the pump barrel. The piston is then inserted into the barrel and operated with the actual jet not attached. Thus tank A and the basin are filled. The jet is then quickly screwed in place and the piston afterwards removed, when the fountain will immediately work. The contributor concludes by pointing out that the fountain could be made bigger for garden purposes and after burying in the ground, a small cement pond could be constructed round it.

Before going on to more elaborate designs the contributor deplores the lack of knowledge of 'hydro-pneumatics' among readers who have raised queries with him, especially those who still think that perpetual motion is a possibility and that therefore a 'self-acting' fountain should play forever. Having written a homily on this, he resumes his description of fountains adapted to different situations.

Fig 150 shows an arrangement of tanks and pipes akin to Rushton's fountain (Fig 148) in which the rubber pipe G, on the left of the basin, is used to blow in air and is then disconnected. There is however an improvement here, for if pipe C is made as wide as convenient, the effort needed to raise water from A to B is much diminished. Fig 151 illustrates the way in which a fountain can be added to a rectangular aquarium supported on a shelf. The action is identical with that in Fig 150, while the pipes in the aquarium (which acts in the same way as the basin in Fig 150) are concealed by covering them with 'rock work'. The fountain is called into action by blowing through a rubber tube attached temporarily to the left-hand pipe, while operation of the tap A, on the right-hand side of the upper tank obviates the necessity for removing the jet when raising water from floor level.

The arrangement in Fig 152 would have been considered an extremely elegant adornment for a square or rounded bay-window, for in this fountain all the pipework is concealed in a rockery supporting ferns and other plants, the only evidence of a hydraulic system being the pipe C which is again blown into to set the fountain working. If preferred, C can be the barrel of a pump permanently fixed there, and a piston inserted whenever it is desired to raise water from B to A.

Fig 153 shows a simple plan for an aquarium and fountain which can be made on quite a large scale, to play for several hours, thus rendering it suitable for advertising purposes in a window display. It is intended for work with several gallons of water where blowing by mouth or pump would be trouble-some.

Noting that the dotted lines represent flexible rubber tubing, the action is as follows. The aquarium being filled and both taps turned on, the bottom tank fills also. Tap D, below the aquarium, is closed and the tanks interchanged and re-connected. On turning on both tap D and the jet the fountain plays until the upper tank is empty, but, be it noted, the level in the aquarium remains unchanged. To restart the fountain the tanks are interchanged once more. Here, of course, the work needed to raise the water is provided by the physical effort of lifting the tanks instead of lung-power used in blowing.

Finally, Fig 154 shows a combined aquarium, fountain and birdcage. All that seems to be missing is a dog-kennel under the table. It is not really 'self-acting', for the fountain simply works from a reservoir supported by the columns and hidden by the inevitable 'rock-work'. In operation, this reservoir is merely charged by dipping from the aquarium, the level of which therefore fluctuates in use. Rather effectively, the pillars are glass tubes, one of which serves to lead water from the reservoir to the jet.

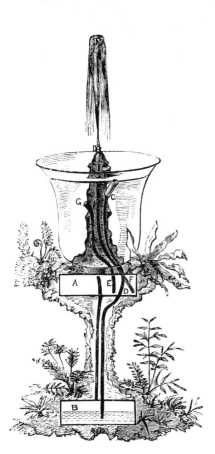

152 Self-acting fountain with aquarium and rockery

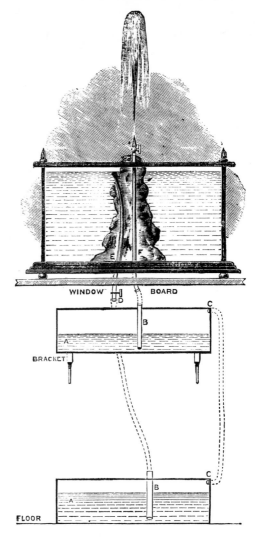

153 Fountain and aquarium suitable for a shop-window display

154 Self-contained aquarium, fountain and birdcage

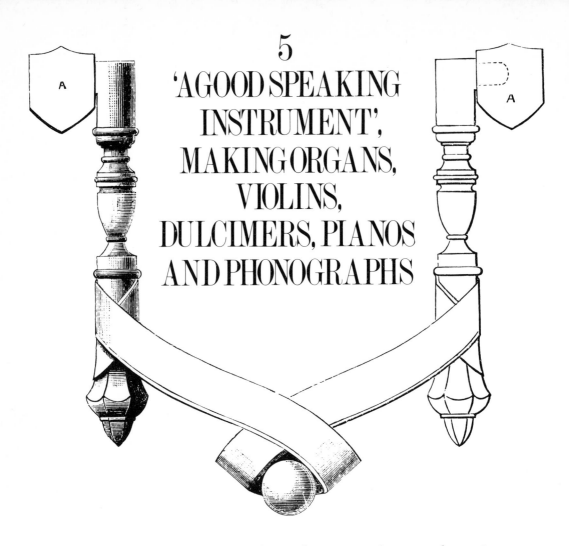

5
'A GOOD SPEAKING INSTRUMENT', MAKING ORGANS, VIOLINS, DULCIMERS, PIANOS AND PHONOGRAPHS

I would advise amateurs not to be in a hurry to get things together, as in this work particularly, hurry is fatal to good results.

Provision for the entertainment of the masses, on the scale we know it today, was non-existent in the last century. London and the larger provincial cities had their theatres and concert halls and alongside these were to be found the music halls devoted to the lighter forms of entertainment—variety shows. But these organised amusements were available only to a fraction of the population

155 Small organ

—the rest of the country had to amuse itself. This it did by indulging in amateur theatricals, music making in the home, choral societies, orchestras and brass bands.

Plenty of amateur talent, of variable quality, was anxious to perform at any charity concert for which an excuse to hold it could be found. Then to the multitude of singers and instrumentalists was added the occasional amateur conjurer, a reciter of sentimental and 'comic' verse, or even a ventriloquist.

Organs

Small Pipe-organ

The very first issue of *Amateur Work* starts a series of articles on making the king of instruments—the organ—albeit a very small chamber model designed to 'discourse sweet music in a drawing room or library, and which may serve as a pleasing accompaniment to the voice of a singer'.

The details of its construction are complicated, but organists will be interested in a few notes on building it. The organ consists of fifty-four pipes, with one manual, no pedals and, of course, no stops. Its scope is therefore limited.

The compass of the instrument is from CC to 'F in alto'. It is suggested that the metal pipes be purchased, new or secondhand, while the amateur is provided with complete instructions for making up a scale whereby the dimensions of all the wooden pipes can be worked out. Indeed, if difficulty is experienced in getting metal pipes he could make all the pipes of wood, though the tonal quality of the instrument would then be quite different.

Fig 155 shows the instrument complete, while Figs 156 and 157 give alternative arrangements of the pipes. Having no pedal board, the organist is expected to blow his instrument himself by the pedal shown in Fig 155. Surely this is an uncommon method of operating the bellows?

We are told that two or three skins of white sheep-leather will be needed for the bellows and that 'druggists keep an excellent quality of it for the purpose of making adhesive plasters'.

Vehicle moved by Spring

JACK writes: I am anxious to get a light vehicle built, say about 56 lbs weight, to carry two persons 12 stone [168lb] each. Would anyone kindly inform me could such a vehicle be driven by the action of a spring, working on the same principle as a watch or clock?

STADT DRESDEN writes: In reply to JACK, I had in mind a patent spring-driven tricycle, the two springs of which cost £10. The machine when tried realized about 8 miles an hour, but required re-winding every 2000 metres. (Kindly give name of tricycle and maker.—Ed.)

JACK writes: Will STADT DRESDEN kindly give the necessary instructions for building the vehicle?

STADT DRESDEN writes: I am unable to give the information you ask. At the time I saw the vehicle (about nine months ago) I looked upon it as an expensive joke rather than a useful article. ... The machine as I saw it was a very crude contrivance, the driving gear was simply a pair of magnified clock-spring barrels about 12 inches in diameter, each having a chain wheel at one edge ... The springs were wound by a pinion engaging in a pair of large wheels, but I thought it a great disadvantage to have to dismount to do so. [I have no doubt of this!] The weight of the machine complete was 300 pounds.

If JACK will take my advice he will let 'the vehicle moved by springs' alone altogether.—Ed.

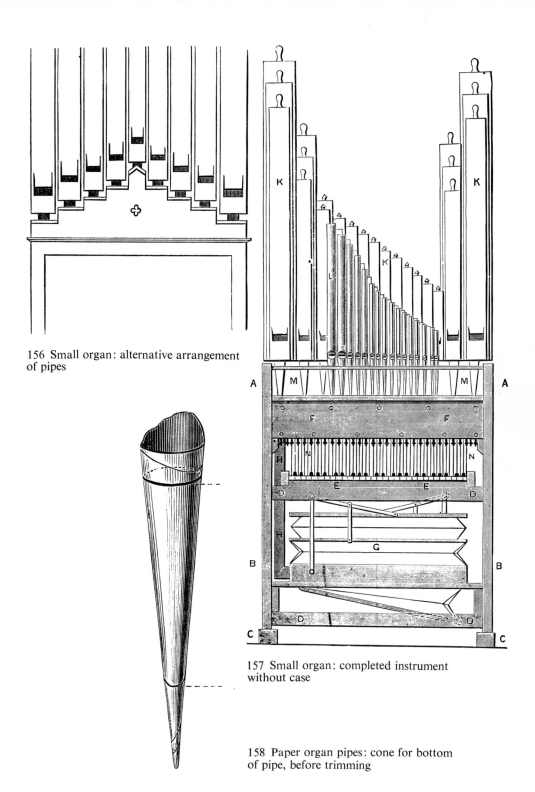

156 Small organ: alternative arrangement of pipes

157 Small organ: completed instrument without case

158 Paper organ pipes: cone for bottom of pipe, before trimming

159 Paper organ pipes: upper languid

160 Paper organ pipes: lower languid

162 Paper organ pipes: upper lip, of wood

163 Paper organ pipes: lower lip, of wood

161 Paper organ pipes: pipe and foot showing languids in position and holes cut, ready for lips

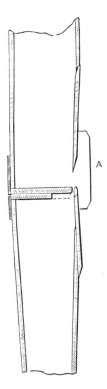

164 Paper organ pipes: complete pipe

165 Paper organ pipes: section of Fig 164

The amateur is not expected to make the keyboard but 'pianofortes are now so common that their cast-off keys are common too'. The instrument will stand 8ft 2in high, so once again a high-pitched room is needed for it to sound well.

Larger Organ with Paper Pipes

A year later (1882) the magazine provides its readers with directions for making a far more ambitious instrument, having 281 pipes enclosed in a general swell-box so that the dimensions of the finished organ are a width of 6ft 6in, height of 9ft and a depth of 3ft.

Specification

1	Open Diapason to Tenor C	44 pipes	8ft
2	Stopped Diapason, Bass	12 pipes	8ft
3	Stopped Diapason, Treble	44 pipes	8ft
4	Flute (for Principal)	56 pipes	4ft
5	Keraulophon (small scale to Tenor C)	44 pipes	2ft
6	Flageolet (for fifteenth)	56 pipes	2ft
7	Bourdon (pedals)	25 pipes	16ft

Couplers: octave; great to pedal

The instrument has therefore one manual with pedals.

This series of articles is remarkable for the method advocated for making pipes of paper. These are to take the place of metal pipes which are far more expensive to produce. Indeed the contributor tells us that a complete stop of paper pipes can be made for about a tenth of the cost of the equivalent in metal. That was in the last century: the difference in cost would now be far greater. The tone is claimed to be quite satisfactory, and, as for strength, paper pipes are much stronger, not being damaged by rough knocks.

This method of making pipes seems so original that I make no apology for giving some details. Each pipe is of paper made into a tube by rolling it round a mandrel, previously prepared by rolling more paper to form a cylinder of the required diameter, determined by a scale of sizes supplied by the contributor. A paper cone (Fig 158) is made and trimmed to size. Languids of correct shape (Figs 159 and 160) are glued to the bottom of the cylinder (upper sketch Fig 161) and to the top of the cone (lower sketch, Fig 161). Lips (Figs 162 and 163) are prepared in wood and fixed in position so that the finished pipe looks like Fig 164, also shown in section in Fig 165. The cylinder at the top slides up and down as a tuning device.

The above description refers to an open pipe, but scales of sizes are provided for all open and stopped pipes needed in this organ.

Several papers follow giving directions for making up the mechanism of the instrument, the bellows, the building frame, manual action, pedal keyboard, stop action, couplers etc. Details of this important and time-consuming work do not concern us here, so we will pass on to the organ case itself, several alternative designs to suit different pipe arrangements being given.

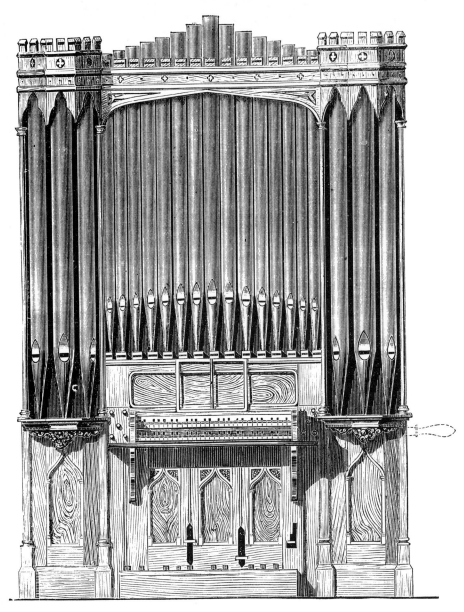

166 Larger organ: two-manual instrument with pedals. Case in 'Tudor' style

Organ Cases

Fig 155 has already shown us the appearance of the small organ first described. Fig 166 is a design for a larger instrument, in a style which the contributor calls 'Tudor . . . to match the furniture of many modern homes'. (He must have had in mind the series of papers on Elizabethan furniture (see Chapter 6).) The general pattern is adaptable to any organ of one or more manuals. The side elevation (Fig 167) emphasises the contributor's liking for exposed pipes—

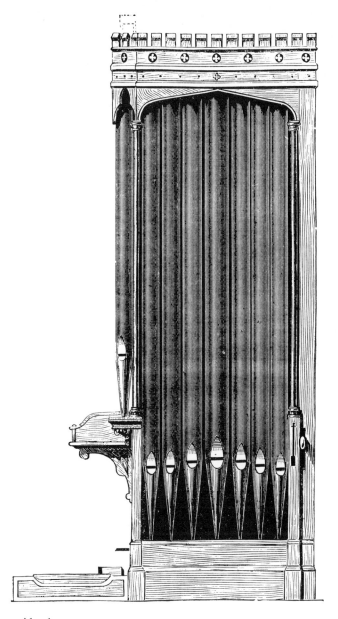

167 Larger organ: side view

speaking ones, not dummies. The handle for hand-blowing is also conspicuous.
Fig 168 is a design for a small organ, blown by the feet of the organist, while
Fig 169 shows the front elevation of a larger instrument suited to the music
gallery of a large mansion or even for a small church. From these suggestions
the amateur was expected to produce a design for his organ case appropriate to
the situation in which it was to stand.

95

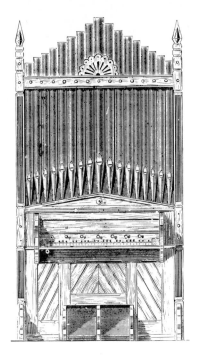

168 Small organ: single manual instrument with bellows blown by foot-boards as in a harmonium

169 Larger organ: alternative design for a case

Dulcimer

From the letters which later appeared in *Amateurs in Council* we know that a single article on dulcimer-making, which appeared in 1882, proved interesting to a number of readers. Fig 170 gives a general view of the instrument which merely consisted of a shallow box of hardwood with a back and belly of pine.

Inside the instrument are other bridges immediately under the ones seen on top, the middle wooden bridge dividing the length of the strings in the ratio of 2 : 3 so that the strings on the left-hand side sound four notes higher than those on the right. The sets of three strings are for natural tones, the sets of two strings providing semi-tones. The hammers (Fig 171) are made of split cane tipped with cork covered with wash-leather.

This instrument was intended mainly for the interest of the solo performer in his own home, but a questioner in the correspondence column of the magazine appears to have heard a public performance on some kind of xylophone which he confuses with a dulcimer, for he writes:

I have several times heard performances upon a kind of dulcimer (I should say it is American from its nature), made of pieces of pine wood laid upon straw, and played with hammers. Could any reader of AMATEUR WORK give me particulars about the construction and cost of a similar instrument?

I am sorry to say he got no reply to his query.

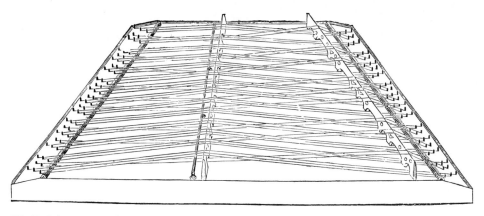

170 Dulcimer: completed instrument

171 Dulcimer: hammer of split cane carrying a cork covered with washleather as a striking piece

Pianoforte

In 1975 Mr Richard Baker, in one of the *Celebration* programmes broadcast on Radio 4, introduced a recital of piano music somewhat as follows: 'Quite a number of amateurs have built pipe-organs, made violins and other members of the string family, but no amateur has ever attempted to make a piano.' Now our magazine seems to give the lie to this remark for in 1888 a series of articles appeared on 'How to make a Piano'. Of course in those days the wooden-framed upright piano was still very commonly in use, but even so it must have been a brave and optimistic craftsman who would attempt such a task. What would induce an amateur to take up the job? Was he really trying to save money, or did he accept this kind of thing as a personal challenge to his craftsmanship, or indeed, pertinacity?

The piano is not really a relative of the clavichord and harpsichord, for the piano 'action' simulates, more artistically, the hand-held hammers of the dulcimer of former times. The instructions for making a piano are rather liberally sprinkled with technical terms, but an outline of the scheme to be followed shows how the work was attempted.

The foundation on which all upright pianos are built is called the 'back' and upon the soundness of its construction the endurance of the instrument and its 'standing in tune' in a very great measure depend. We are, of course, thinking of a wooden-frame instrument. Fig 172 shows the front and treble section of a finished 'back'. The strings will ultimately be fixed between the plank B, of

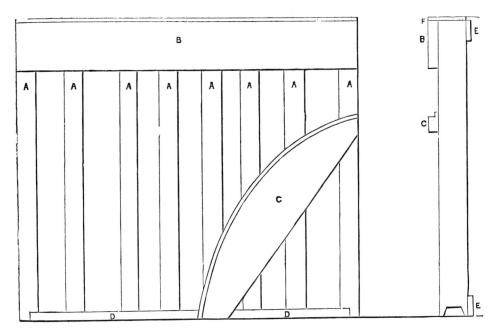

172 Pianoforte: front and treble section of finished 'back' of instrument

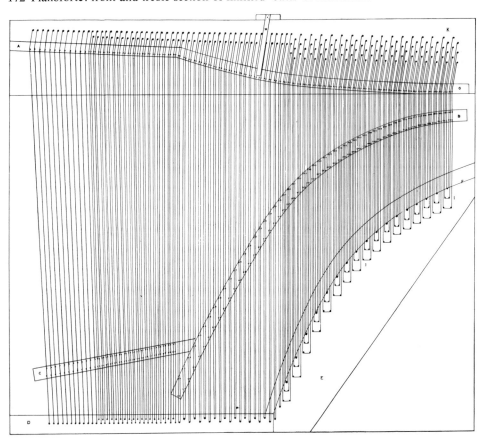

173 Pianoforte: arrangement of stringing

beech, veneered with sycamore, and the bottom piece D, or on to the bent side C.

Fig 173 shows how complicated the stringing operation is going to be, although the 'overstrung' principle is not being used, in spite of the fact that overstringing had been applied to upright pianos as long ago as 1828.

The case is intended to be of solid walnut, and therefore very heavy. Fig 174 shows that the design was traditional. The contributor gives illustrations of three 'actions' (ie the hammer arrangement for striking each note), eighty-five being needed for this eighty-five note instrument. The 'sticker' or 'hopper' action was formerly commonly found in pianos of English manufacture. Its chief merit was that it would keep in order for many years, but if struck hard, the hammer would strike the string twice. The Molyneaux action was very popular at one time for it incorporated a check to prevent the hammer rebounding and striking the string again. It was also extremely durable.

The tape, crank, or French action was greatly preferred by the contributor. It is really of English origin, the invention of Robert Wornum, but not being taken up by English makers it passed over to the Continent where it was used almost exclusively, returning to England in pianos of foreign origin. Its

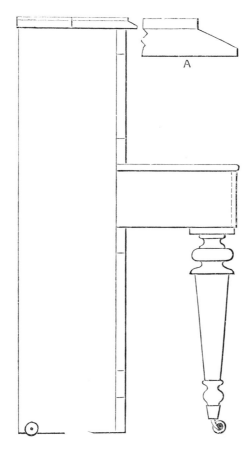

174 Pianoforte: side view of walnut case

advantage was that it was of good lasting quality and incorporated a check action which engaged the hammer immediately the blow was struck, preventing it striking again until the key was released. It was also beautifully sensitive and responsive to the touch. All three actions are shown in Figs 175, 176 and 177.

Having explained the operation of an 'action' the contributor cheats a bit and asks the constructor to buy his 'action' and keys from a manufacturer but even if this were done, all eighty-five 'actions' and keys had to be properly aligned and fixed on rails to produce the correct note in every case—a formidable task.

The building of the piano was completed when the pedal mechanism had been added.

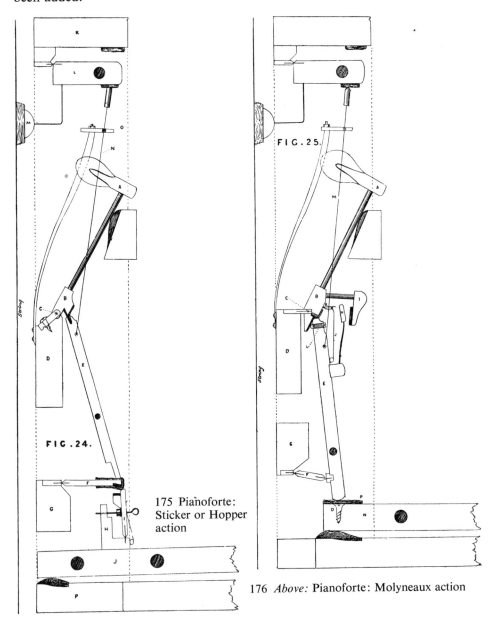

FIG.24.

175 Pianoforte: Sticker or Hopper action

FIG.25.

176 *Above:* Pianoforte: Molyneaux action

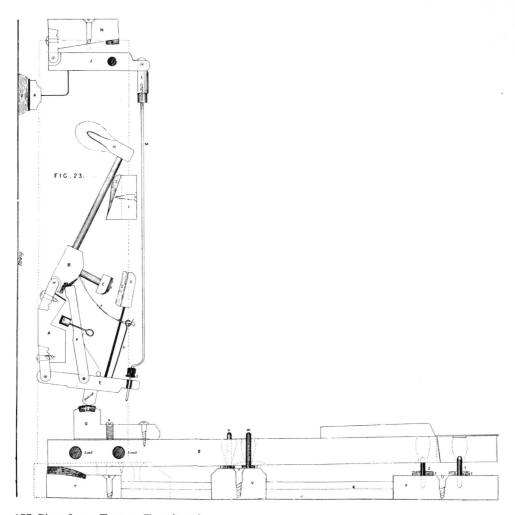

FIG. 23.

177 Pianoforte: Tape or French action

Aeolian Harp

The Aeolian harp is another example of something quaint and unusual which tickled the fancy of the Victorian householder. The name is derived from Aeolus who had charge of the winds in ancient mythology and perhaps this instrument is intended when the Talmudical record states that the Kinnor, or David's harp, sounded of itself when the wind blew upon it. However, the modern form of the instrument must be credited to Athanasius Kircher, born at Geysen in 1602.

Fig 178 shows a plan of the harp, while Fig 179 is a section of the same. From these two diagrams it can be seen that the instrument consists of a long shallow box over which strings are stretched. Sound holes are cut as shown in Fig 178.

The steel pins at one end for attaching the strings are the same as those used in a piano, while the tuning pegs at the opposite end are the ordinary wooden pegs of a violin. The strings may be of catgut, steel, or brass and can be of any

101

178 Aeolian harp: plan

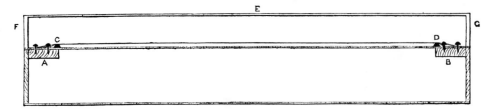

179 Aeolian harp: section

number—more giving greater sound. A kind of roof, open at the sides (Fig 179), is fastened above the strings to allow air to blow over them when the harp is placed in an open window, the bottom sash being lowered on to this roof. We are told that the strings are usually all tuned to the orchestral 'A'.

Double-acting Aeolian Harp

Fig 180 shows a more sophisticated model of such a harp, called by the designer a 'double-acting Aeolian harp'. In effect, it is two harps placed top and bottom of a long box, though in the diagram, the top harp, being under the lid, is not visible. A further refinement is obtained by making each harp slope from the outside of the window towards the inside, so that when the box is placed under the sash the wind can funnel into the room rather than flow smoothly over the strings. Again, the box should be the exact length of the window into which it is fitted so that all the air entering the room passes over the strings. This contributor is a little more economical with the materials for his pegs, for French nails are suggested for the fixed end, while ordinary round-headed screws suffice as tuning pegs at the other.

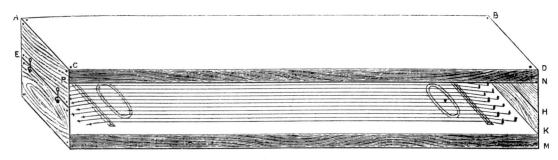

180 Double-acting Aeolian harp

Dumb Violin

Not only jerry-built, twentieth-century houses are provided with walls so thin that everything happening next door may be heard, for in 1882 a contributor from New South Wales writes feelingly:

I am an enthusiastic lover of music and am an amateur violinist, but I have to work for my living; and in my present situation I live in the house which also contains my employer, his wife and two children. The children go to bed early, and consequently, *though I am free from 9 pm* I cannot practise as my room adjoins theirs, and in the early morning my employer does not like to be awakened before 8 am and at that time I start work, so all my available practice time was of no use to me.

Note that this contributor was working thirteen hours a day and yet tried to practise a hobby!

He was so anxious to play that he stuffed spare clothing against the door, plugged up the key-hole and tried playing his violin with a bow without resin on it, but still he could be heard in the adjoining bedroom. Finally, he thought of making a dumb violin—that is, a violin of solid wood not resounding much to the vibration of the strings. He made this by first cutting out a paper pattern from the back of his real violin. This he stuck to a block of pinewood, cutting out the shape as in Fig 181, but altering the shape of the inner bouts to reduce the weight somewhat. This body was next rounded off to resemble the general shape of his violin. The scroll and peg-box (Fig 182) caused him some concern for he was afraid that, being of pinewood, the peg-box would not stand the strain of the stretched strings, but his luck held. However:

My next difficulty was a fingerboard. I went to our town music seller's, and after a deal of fossicking, a violin was found which had been sat on and had suffered in the belly in consequence. By the persuasive eloquence of the large blade of a penknife, that fingerboard was induced to part company from its body, and I took it home in triumph.

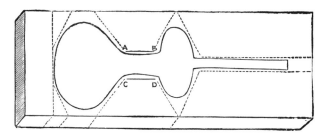

181 Dumb violin: pattern marked out on block of pine wood

Right:
182 Dumb violin: scroll and peg-box

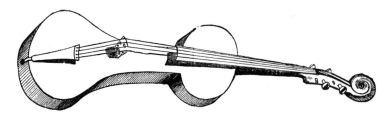

183 Dumb violin: finished instrument

Eventually he added a tail-piece, nut and bridge, and Fig 183 shows the rather odd shape of the finished instrument.

> The tone of my violin was peculiar. It sounded to me and my musical friends as though a fly were imprisoned near their ear. When I shut my door now, I can practise to my heart's content, and unless anyone stops and listens by my door, they can hear nothing.

What a triumph of ingenuity over difficulties.

Bagpipes

In the correspondence columns a gentleman from Orkney asks how to make a set of bagpipes. Curiously, the first reply came from Rugby in England, but perhaps the correspondent was an ex-patriot Scot. For the pipes, cocoa-wood or ebony is essential, he says, but another writer from Co Cavan in Ireland says that whitethorn, apple, or cherry will do. All correspondents who replied to the Orcadian assumed that he had a lathe on which to turn his drones and chanter.

The subject became even more involved when a correspondent using the pseudonym Peterofsky asked:

> Can any of 'ours' tell me how to make a set of Irish (Query: Scotch. Ed.) Bagpipes? I should make the drones of brass piping, but don't know how the mouthpiece, or whatever it is which makes the sound, is made.

Surely it is extraordinary that anyone, with such a sketchy idea of what a set of bagpipes looked like, should embark on their construction and think of using brass for the drones.

Simple Banjo

The banjo probably reached the zenith of its popularity in the last two decades of the nineteenth century. It originated in North America and was of course long associated with 'Nigger Minstrels, blackened faces, *et hoc genus omne*'.

But an interest in the instrument did not die easily, for a revival took place in the early 1920s when no 'jazz band' was properly equipped without its banjo, and that *virtuoso* of the instrument, Mario de Pietro, was one of the most popular solo performers on 'the wireless' in front of the microphone at the Savoy Hill studios of the BBC. A school friend of mine, who to the ears of his fellow pupils rivalled Mario de Pietro in expertise, playing, as he did, much the same repertoire, amassed sufficient funds by his banjo playing during the weekends to pay his college fees in the days when students' grants were almost non-existent, and in any case minute in quantity.

The instrument consists of a handle and a hoop. The handle, of walnut, can be cut out in one piece as shown in the side view Fig 184 and from the top in Fig 185. Fig 186 is a front view of the complete instrument showing how five strings are stretched the full length of the handle while a peg at A accommodates a shorter sixth string. Banjos can have five, six or seven strings, but the contributor favours six.

184 Simple banjo: block of walnut marked out for the handle—front view

185 Simple banjo: block of walnut marked out for the handle—side view

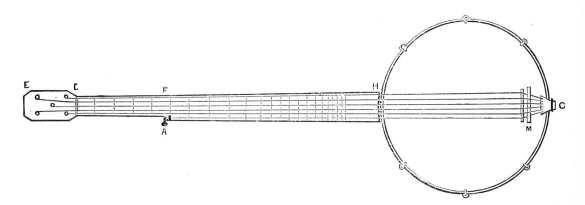

186 Simple banjo: front view of instrument with strings

Making the hoop is of course the most difficult part of the construction. It is made of a strip of oak ¼in thick, 2½in wide and about 37in long. After suitable steaming to render the wood pliable, it is bent into a hoop some 11in in diameter and the bevelled ends screwed together to make a neat join. A second hoop, or band, only ½in wide, is made to slip over the first. A circle of iron wire must next be made to slip over the first hoop to keep the parchment drum-like surface in place. The narrow band of oak is then added to give a good tension all round and this is fastened by twelve special clamps which must be bought.

The bridge and pegs, best made of box wood, show up clearly in Fig 187. The six strings may then be fixed in place and the instrument is now ready for tuning.

This first article on banjo-making initiated some correspondence in which the writer justified the recommending of a wooden hoop in preference to the more elegant brass model because 'of a request for a paper on Banjo-making from a reader in some out-of-the-way place in Florida; and thinking there might be more such, I was induced to recommend a wooden rim'.

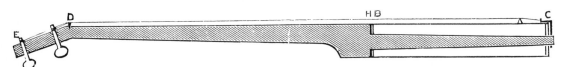

187 Simple banjo: section of the completed instrument

Improved Banjo

Fig 188 shows the instrument described in the contributor's second paper. The handle, again of walnut, is to be faced with rosewood or ebony. In this case the hoop is still of oak but covered with thin sheet brass. The bridge and tail-piece are of ivory. The number of clamps is increased to twenty-four or even to thirty-six if preferred, to give a more even tension to the vellum used for the drum. Frets are located on the handle to ensure the production of accurate notes and the stars and diamonds, shown in Fig 189, by indicating the different 'positions', are of great assistance in playing.

A correspondent who had actually tried to make one of these instruments found difficulty in bending the wood for his hoop, because

> the operation is not so easy as it looks, and the following is how I escaped it:—I got from a wire worker a sieve rim, before it had been wired, for a few pence. It was made of beech, just the right thickness, and about $\frac{1}{2}$ inch too broad, already jointed, but not joined, and bent to the circle. I perfected the joint, glued and screwed it, and when I had gauged and ripped it to the correct breadth, I had a first-class rim with very little trouble and expense.

Just one more example of Victorian ingenuity.

An Extraordinary Wind Instrument

The most extraordinary instrument to be found in these magazines was described in an issue in 1888 and is illustrated in operation in Fig 190. The 'common household bellows' was indeed common in the nineteenth century for 'coaxing a weakly fire into burning briskly', so that this musical (?) instrument must be the cheapest to make in this series of papers, for nothing else is needed except the human mouth. Playing it sounds a thoroughly unhygienic pastime for surely

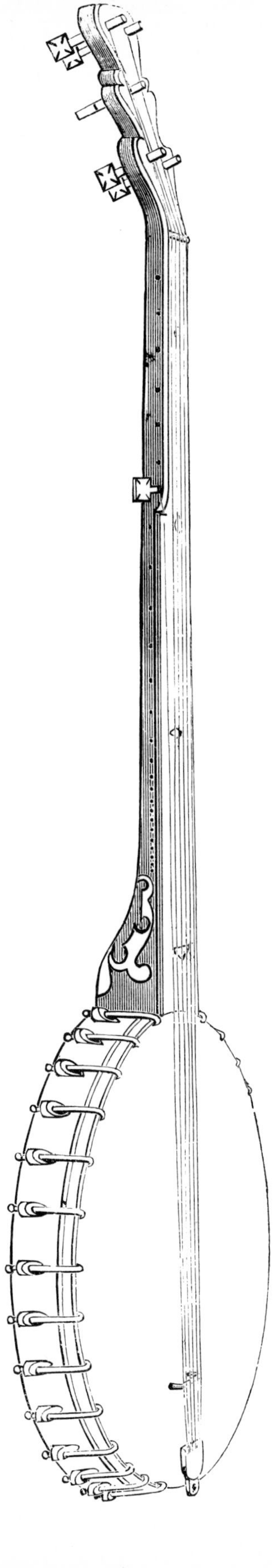

188 Banjo of superior quality: complete

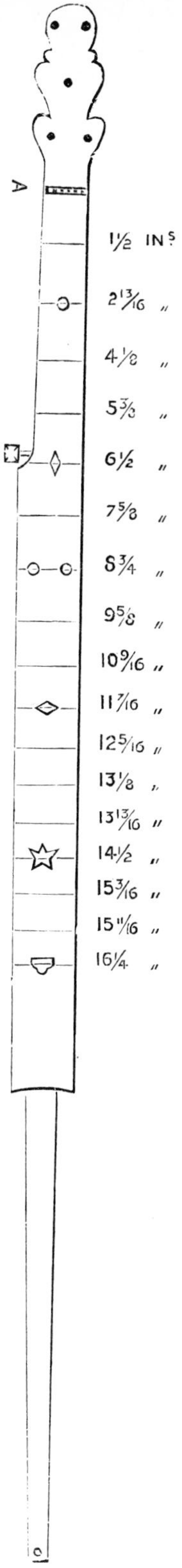
A
1½ INS.
2 13/16 "
4 1/8 "
5 3/8 "
6½ "
7 5/8 "
8¾ "
9 5/8 "
10 9/16 "
11 7/16 "
12 5/16 "
13 1/8 "
13 13/16 "
14½ "
15 3/16 "
15 11/16 "
16¼ "

189 Banjo of superior quality: position of frets on the handle

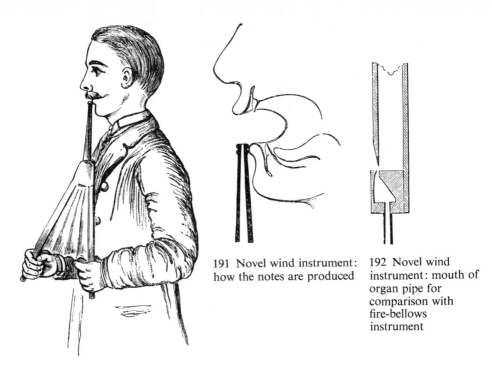

191 Novel wind instrument: how the notes are produced

192 Novel wind instrument: mouth of organ pipe for comparison with fire-bellows instrument

190 Novel wind instrument: fire bellows

dust from the bellows would be blown directly into the mouth, but the contributor makes no comment on this.

A comparison of Fig 191 with Fig 192 at once shows that the relationship between mouth and bellows is to be likened to that of the wind coming from an organ bellows and hitting the lip of an organ pipe. We are assured that if the bellows are worked while held as in Fig 190, the note produced will resemble that of a flute. The pitch of the note we get is to be controlled by altering the shape and position of the lips, the size of the mouth cavity, by tongue movements and by blowing harder with the bellows. A bellows with a $\frac{1}{4}$in nozzle is capable of giving a range of notes extending 'three octaves upwards from G on the fourth space of the bass clef'.

The contributor found that his performance on this instrument was inclined (surely an understatement) to amuse as well as fascinate his audience and warns us that 'a little effort is required to refrain from laughing with your audience'. Apparently he gave solo performances with piano accompaniment and eventually attained such skill that, with the inner handle of the bellows strapped to his chest and the outer handle operated by one hand, he could accompany himself with the other.

He was so carried away with enthusiasm for his invention that he devised a method of executing intricate slurs, by altering the mouth and lip movements during one 'blow' from the bellows. Staccato playing was achieved by 'hitting the outer handle as rapidly as may be required with the heel of the right hand' and shakes could be effected by suitable manipulation of the tongue and mouth.

If alive today the contributor could surely join those radio performers who sometimes regale us with 'music' on hose-pipes and watering-cans.

Phonograph

I have already referred to the frequency with which some clergy were fascinated by the more recreational aspects of experimental science. A clerical contributor had already written several papers on making scientific apparatus and in 1888 included a single article on the construction of a phonograph which had been patented ten years before by the prolific American inventor, Thomas Alva Edison.

As is so often the case in these articles, the preamble is of considerable historical interest, constantly reminding us how much technological invention took place in the latter half of the nineteenth century. The contributor marvels at the ingenuity of the Bell's telephone (originally used as both mouthpiece and receiver) and the more recent microphone invented by Professor David Hughes

> ... by which we have heard the fly brushing its coat and scraping its feet. But these marvels were eclipsed when Mr. Edison discovered that the human voice ... could be chronicled, and invented a machine by which it could be reproduced!

In his allusion to the microphone the contributor is referring to the very first demonstration of the instrument before Fellows of the Royal Society,

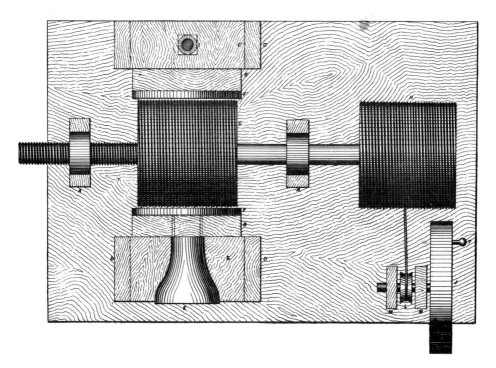

193 Phonograph: plan of instrument

when a fly was actually used to show the extreme sensitivity of the instrument for detecting faint sounds, far surpassing the Bell telephone for this purpose. The contributor recalls the impact of Edison's invention on journalists in the late 1870s and how the phonograph would enable future generations to listen to voices of long ago.

The principle on which the phonograph worked will be familiar to most readers, the general idea being that a metal cylinder, C in Fig 193, is caused to move from left to right on a spindle which is grooved to the same pitch as a groove cut in the large cylinder itself. A second cylinder H, of wood, but otherwise identical to C is carried on the right-hand end of the spindle. This also is grooved like C. The contributor arranged a small pulley wheel L, on nearby supports, driven by turning the handle T on the heavy metal wheel J. This pulley was coupled to the cylinder H by a gut band. On turning the handle the cylinder C could be caused to rotate and at the same time travel smoothly from one end of the machine towards the other. This ingenious device was used to make it easier to rotate the cylinder at a more or less constant speed—an essential requirement for good sound reproduction as all users of gramophones and tape-recorders will appreciate. By rotating the wheel J at about four revolutions per second, the spindle and main cylinder moved at about one revolution per second which was the speed desired.

E is the receiver or recording mouthpiece. Essentially it consists of a strong piece of mahogany with a hole in it, 3in in diameter. Over the hole is clamped a thin sheet of ferrotype—thin iron highly enamelled on one side and formerly much used by photographers for glazing prints. From the centre of this disc protrudes a blunt steel point, made from a knitting needle or large darning needle. This is shown in Fig 194.

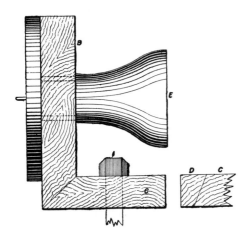

194 Phonograph: side view of recorder

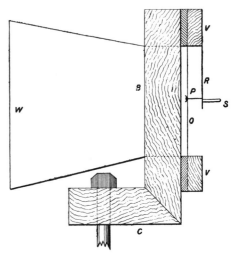

195 Phonograph: side view of repeater or reproducer

The reproducer or repeater (Fig 195) is mounted on the opposite side of the main cylinder and is constructed rather differently, for in this case the diaphragm O is of stiff parchment coupled to a stylus S attached to a piece of watch spring R, the coupling being of strong sewing silk. Using this form of coupling, the stylus could move in and out but not laterally. W is a small paper cone or horn.

To operate the machine, the main cylinder is smoothly covered with a sheet of tinfoil, gummed in place. The crank is rotated, bringing the cylinder to the right, and the position of the recorder is adjusted until its stylus makes a faint indentation in the foil. The reproducer is of course clear of the cylinder.

Now let someone speak into the mouthpiece, distinctly, not shouting. Try first with some well known rhyme [as did Edison with 'Mary had a little lamb'], then sing some familiar ditty.

The recorder is next drawn back and the cylinder rotated to its first position. Next the reproducer is adjusted until its stylus fits in a tinfoil groove when the rhyme and song will be repeated.

But you must take it for granted that you will not succeed the first time; some little while will elapse before the knack and knowledge are acquired. However, if the instructions are followed out strictly, a good speaking instrument will result.

The tinfoil phonograph was far too fragile to attain great success so that it was not until the sound track was cut in a wax cylinder that acceptable quality of reproduction was obtained.

6
'THE ARMS OF THE MASTER OF THE HOUSE', REPRODUCTION ELIZABETHAN FURNITURE AND HERALDIC DECORATION

We may be sure that a man who shows pride in his ancestors will be less likely than another to disgrace their name and his own by any mean or dishonourable conduct.

Many country clergymen of the last century had plenty of time on their hands to pursue personal interests without neglecting the duties of their office, for almost every parish church had its own resident rector or vicar, or, failing this, a resident curate in place of an absentee occupier of the benefice.

In those days they were usually graduates of Oxford or Cambridge and, more often than not, the only well educated people in rural communities besides doctors or lawyers. Consequently, they tended to have interests which they were unable to share with their parishioners. Quite a number of parish clergy made useful contributions to the sum total of knowledge in the sciences at a time when the amateur needed no elaborate laboratory or expensive apparatus to equip himself to make worthwhile discoveries in astronomy, botany or geology. Others with a mechanical bent were able to cultivate their skill in various crafts, sometimes linking these with the physical sciences to produce apparatus for simple demonstrations in optics and electricity with which to instruct, or perhaps mystify, their parishioners. Not a few made 'magic lanterns' —similar to modern slide-projectors—and painted glass lantern slides to use with them, for the photographic production of slides was not yet widely practised. Others practised craftsmanship for the sheer beauty of the results produced in wood, ivory, metal, or other materials.

Elizabethan Work

Thus we find several clergymen among the contributors to *Amateur Work*. One such has supplied a series of articles on Elizabethan furniture and its reproduction, a term which he uses to refer to the construction of oak furniture in the 'Elizabethan' style, using the word rather loosely to include designs in favour between, say, 1540 and 1650, covering what we sometimes call Stuart or Jacobean, in addition to patterns developed from true Elizabethan furniture.

'Elizabethan' is therefore used in a rather wide sense in this series to describe domestic woodwork of the sixteenth and seventeenth centuries. Architecturally, the Gothic revival precedes the period covered by these magazines, but an interest in all things Gothic, such as architecture, heraldry and stained glass persisted intermittently for almost a hundred years. Indeed, as far as furniture is concerned, a further Gothic revival in the 1870s might account for articles on the reproduction of Gothic styles appearing in the 1880s. C. L. Eastlake writing in his *Hints on Household Taste* in 1878 refers to the prevalence of faked oak furniture to be found in the curiosity shops of Wardour Street (in London's Soho district) and our contributor also comments sarcastically on 'Wardour Street oak'.

China Cabinet

Fig 196 shows an Elizabethan cabinet rather overloaded with blue and white china—a craze of the time. The contributor suggests that we use this piece of furniture as a model for a similar cabinet to be made from such secondhand oak as is available. To encourage the would-be constructor Fig 197 and Fig 198 give front and side elevations of a cabinet made by the contributor in just this way.

Use of Old Oak

It is very clear that this clerical contributor had much storage space available and possessed more than average skill in cabinet-making. It would seem that old four-poster beds, now worth a fortune, could be picked up for a song, while acres of oak panelling and dozens of oak chests were freely to be had. He tells us how he picked up such items in country houses but omits to mention another possible source of material, to wit, the box-pews and galleries then being removed from churches up and down the country.

Regarding bedsteads, we are told that 'I demolished one not long ago, and under the magician's wand of bench and tools, transformed it into a fine old cabinet [Fig 196] which looked like the genuine work of two hundred and fifty years ago.'

196 Reproduction Elizabethan cabinet with nineteenth-century blue china

197 Cabinet made from old pieces of carved oak

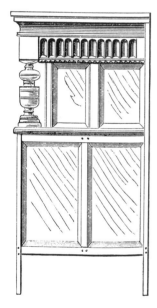

198 Side view of the cabinet
in Fig 197

Right:
199 Bedpost suitable for use in
making reproduction Elizabethan
furniture

200 Another bedpost suitable
for conversion

In Figs 199 and 200 we have illustrations of carved bedposts which can be adapted for other purposes while the panelling of Fig 201 and the cornice in Fig 202 can be used in almost any cabinet or buffet sideboard such as Fig 203. Panels from a finely carved chest (Fig 204) could be particularly useful.

201 Old oak panelling suitable for construction
of reproduction furniture

202 Cornice from an old oak bedstead

203 Reproduction court cupboard or buffet

204 Finely carved chest: panels from this can be used in reproduction work

205 Gothic cabinet: design by Pugin

Designs by Pugin

To demonstrate to the really ambitious craftsman what can be produced, sketches of two designs by Pugin are shown in Figs 205 and 206. Augustus Welby Northmore Pugin (1812–52), the famous Victorian architect, collaborated with R. Akerman in publishing four volumes of Gothic designs for furniture, metalwork and house decoration. These were notable for their authentic detail but the overall effect certainly does not appeal to the modern collector. By 1835 he was already working with that other well known architect, Charles Barry, and between 1840 and 1844 was responsible for the decorations of the chamber of the new House of Lords, the old Palace of Westminster having been destroyed by fire in 1834. Barry's design for the new Palace of Westminster (the Houses of Parliament) was not to be completed until 1867, though Pugin continued to help him until his early death.

The austere design of the very heavy Tudor cradle in Fig 207 indicates that it is copied from a model of 1500 or thereabouts, but it does not look particularly convenient or hygienic.

206 Gothic bedstead: design by Pugin

207 Tudor cradle: a reproduction

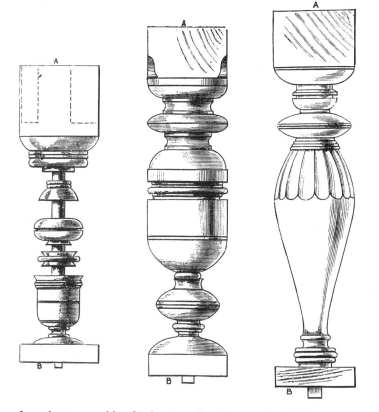

208 Three designs for columns capable of being turned on the amateur's lathe

A very complete workshop must have been available, for we are told to turn up, on the lathe, columns for our cabinet from portions of bedposts, or even from beams if no suitable posts are at hand. Suggested patterns are shown in Fig 208.

As an alternative, old table legs might be cut down. Considerable skill as a woodworker was needed to produce cornices like those shown in section in Fig 209, though the writer dismisses the subject rather lightly:

Having selected our wood, the task before us is one rather of labour than skill, though a certain amount of this is needful for obtaining a true curve and we must go on working with our hollowing plane till the required depth has been reached.

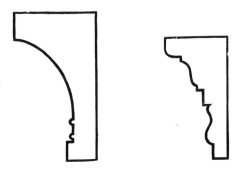

209 Two designs for cornices for a cabinet

When all the parts of the cabinet were completed the most interesting decorative work had still to be done—and there could be much of this needed if the old oak to hand was not of suitable design. For example, if the carved panels available were insufficient to complete the cabinet, further matching panels had to be carved. If panels had to be completely redesigned, a suitable pattern is given in Fig 210. All the rails and stiles had to have mouldings along each edge and sections of forms often found in old furniture are offered to the constructor in Fig 211.

Fig 212 shows designs suitable for the perpendicular side rails or legs of the lower part. Figs 213 and 214 show thumb and other carving appropriate to the upper front and side rails. Hinges and handles must of course be in keeping and Fig 215 gives designs for these items.

Stains were used to bring all the pieces of oak to one colour before fixing together. Putting on the finest oil polish completed the work.

Old Oak Chests

Before going on to further designs the contributor gives some account of his experiences when hunting up old oak. Collectors of antiques were not unknown in late Victorian times and consequently dealers were also active in snapping up the best items of oak furniture, but old corner cupboards, dressers, carved boxes, chests and tables could result from careful search. Ancient chests were

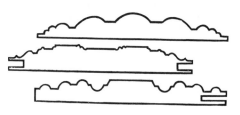

211 Cross-sections of rails in old furniture which the amateur could copy for his reproductions

213 Traditional thumb carving for the upper front and side rails of a cabinet

210 Design for a panel of a cabinet

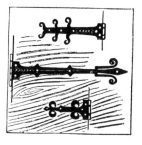

214 Alternative pattern for the upper front and side rails of a cabinet

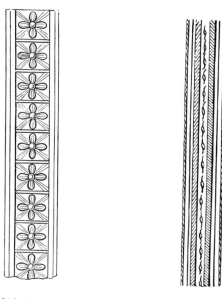

212 Suggestions for the carving of side rails or the legs of a cabinet

215 Hinges and handles for Elizabethan furniture

particularly desirable, as they provided wood in shapes eminently suitable for adaptation to other purposes. Occasionally these chests were too well decorated for sacrifice to other uses. The contributor located one such, doing duty as a corn bin in a wayside inn in Devonshire but which eventually found its way to the rooms of an Oxford don. Bearing all this in mind, the contributor reminds the intending purchaser, 'if in search of chests, to buy them if he can, *in loco penatium*'.

Fig 216 shows a small chest so altered as to form a flower stand. If the amateur is a competent lathe-worker, he can produce a stand with turned legs as shown here, but if this is thought to be too elaborate, a simpler plan is suggested in Fig 217. Even in this case, '. . . before the stand is finally fastened together, the end and side rails must be carved, moulded or inlaid, according to the character of the chest'.

If the chosen chest still has its lid, or perhaps lock, these must be removed and all traces of this workmanship obliterated, inserting a piece of old oak where the iron lock and plate once did good service, carving the added wood to match the rest of the rail. An inner case of ordinary white wood must be made to stand

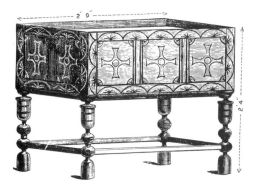

217 Simple support for the flower stand if the amateur has no access to a lathe

216 Small chest adapted to form a flower stand

218 Chest converted into a small buffet

219 Design for the lid of a small chest

220 Large buffet made from a chest and pieces from tables, bedsteads and panelling

in the chest and this again may contain a zinc tray to catch drainage from the pot plants the chest is now expected to hold. Finally the wood must be well rubbed with oil and dry polished with a brush.

Fig 218 shows a different way of utilising an old chest. If mounted on a suitable stand (in this case turned on the lathe and carved), doors substituted for one side and the top secured permanently, we have a buffet or cabinet, the inside of which can be adapted to take dishes, glasses or bottle racks. The top can be left smooth to carry a vase of flowers or to support a potted aspidistra, or it may become an ornament in its own right by being carved as in Fig 219. It should be noted that this design incorporates the constructor's initials and carries an heraldic motif (see also p 127). Instead of using this piece of furniture as a buffet it can easily be converted into a music Canterbury by placing vertical divisions inside rather as we would have in a record cabinet.

Large Buffet

Fig 220 shows a more imposing piece of furniture made up of a moderate sized chest round which the rest of the buffet is built. The columns can be made from table legs or adapted from bedposts while the carved backpiece is put together from available panelling. Much moulding and carving is indicated on the canopy, again presupposing considerable skill on the part of the amateur. The small chest underneath is a fine specimen of a deed box.

Figs 221, 222 and 223 are admittedly not pure examples of characteristic work of any definite period but are of sufficiently attractive appearance to be offered to the amateur as models to be copied by the more skilful and enthusiastic cabinet-maker.

Settle

The settle (Fig 221), the contributor admits, has obviously been modified, if indeed it ever saw 'those so-called good old days!' A feature is the drawer underneath, the handles being carved in the form of leopards' heads. The mermaids under the legend 'Welcome Home' are furnished with combs and mirrors as if about to perform their mid-ocean toilet. This centre panel is flanked by others showing a ship on the left and two churches on the right. Elizabethan interpretations of the Caryatides support the cornice. This portion

221 Carved oak settle

of the settle may well be genuine, for an interest in Grecian design was growing in the late sixteenth century. The centre of the cornice carries a griffin flanked by well executed scallop shells. The arms of the settle are embellished with sea-serpents. After sketching in outline some ideas for the construction of this piece of furniture the contributor admits that by its size and weight it is really only fitted for 'a room of large dimensions or a spacious hall'.

Corner Cupboard

The corner cupboard (Fig 222) is more easily reproduced for a room of moderate size and, perhaps, is not quite so difficult to construct. The design is such that much of the carving can be done on comparatively small pieces of wood, the whole being fitted together later. This would be easier than working on massive boards. It is suggested that the shelving should be covered with old gold-figured velvet and, after bringing all the woodwork to a uniform colour, bees-wax will bring up a suitable polish.

222 Carved oak
corner cupboard

125

223 Oak cabinet derived from a court cupboard design

Large Cabinet

The massive cabinet (Fig 223) is admitted as bearing indications of the late nineteenth-century designer, though much of the carving is genuinely old. The general design shows that it is a descendant of the 'court' cupboard—a cupboard produced at the same time as the large oak presses still occasionally to be found. The original court cupboard was for the display of plate and also functioned to some extent as a sideboard. Sixteenth-century court cupboards were in oak, as in this design, but similar cupboards were later made in walnut.

In the original, from which this drawing was made, the carving was uniformly of excellent quality. Some inlay has been introduced in the doors among much intricate carving. The would-be imitator is reminded that the doors of the cabinet proper include the whole of the two top panels: panels, arches and columns swinging open on posts behind the two end figures. This method of opening seems based upon later Jacobean work, and gives freer access to the interior than would be the case if the inlaid panels only, under the arches, were free to open, though this would be more in keeping with earlier Elizabethan practice. The supports on which the cabinet rests are clearly from old table

126

legs. The remainder of the very elaborate decoration must have been most carefully selected and connecting portions meticulously designed and executed.

In leaving this final example of oak furniture before the reader the contributor hopes, 'the work done will serve as an unfailing incentive to fresh efforts and the preliminary to even greater triumphs'.

Heraldry in Design

The revival of interest in Elizabethan and Gothic features in the late Victorian age was accompanied by a liberal use of armorial decoration in keeping with the use of heraldic devices for ornamental purposes during the reign of the first Elizabeth. Our magazine therefore, not altogether surprisingly, carries a series of papers on the use of heraldry in the aggrandisement not only of the structure of the house, but also in connection with interior decoration and furnishings generally.

In spite of the general interest in heraldry the contributor evidently felt some apology was needed, in case, in the opinion of some of his readers, the display of heraldic devices smacked too much of ostentation,

> ... and a desire to assert the importance of one's family. But family pride may have its good side. ... When a man is proud of his ancestry, and shows it by displaying their armorial symbols, it by no means follows that he is a cockscomb, who holds all such as can adduce no such honours in contempt.

Heraldic Chandelier

A heraldic chandelier (Fig 224) was thought to be a suitable adjunct to a dining room furnished in the Elizabethan style and, if triangular in shape, as shown in plan in Fig 225, this could appropriately carry the arms of the owner's family,

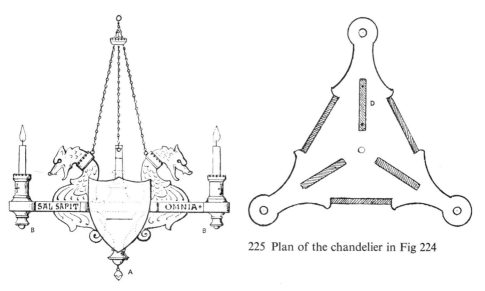

225 Plan of the chandelier in Fig 224

224 Chandelier for a dining room

his university and college. The heraldic monsters, carrying the brass suspension chains, are slightly carved, rather than left in silhouette, but if the constructor cannot do this carving, he 'could very well rely on getting this effect afterwards; in colour, and content himself with merely rounding and finishing-off the edges with file and glass paper'.

The final effect is intended to be far from subdued, for in addition to emblazoning the shields, the whole of the woodwork is to be decorated in gold and colour. The monsters are a neutral green, picked out with gold, the edge of the horizontal triangular board carrying the mottoes, is cream edged with vermilion and the lettering itself is black or blue. In the case of the design shown, it is assumed that the amateur worker is a citizen of London and a liveryman of the Salters' Company and that he has used his own family coat of arms with that of the City of London and that of the Salters. The design for one shield (that of the Worshipful Company of Salters) is shown in Fig 226—note the salt-cellars—while their motto, *Sal sapit omnia*, seems particularly fitted to figure over a dining table.

226 Shield for a chandelier: the arms of the Worshipful Company of Salters

Amateur craftsmen who had not the advantage of being liverymen of an ancient city company need not give up hope of finding suitable heraldic arms. The worker might be able to use his own paternal arms with those of his mother and grandmother, or he might wish to use his own shield (I like the firm assumption that all readers of the magazine have one) with that of the town in which he lives, or of which he is a native, or that of some guild or society of which he is a member.

Armorial Cornice

Those who need something on a grander scale are urged to go in for an armorial cornice which would be suitable in a dining-room or hall.

Fig 227 gives an impression of a small section of the finished product complete with shields and motto. It is interesting to note that indirect evidence of the expectation that this decoration would be applied to a lofty room is given by the hint that the shield should be slightly elongated over the traditional proportions 'to allow for foreshortening'.

227 Cornice, with shields, for a dining room

In the case of the dining room which the contributor had in mind, some thirty different shields were erected—'those of the families from which the emblazoner was descended or to which his own had been allied'. Rather naïvely we are told how to overcome a shortage of arms-bearing relatives. One's own arms can be placed alternatively between shields bearing the arms of one's connections—'this will save the finding of one half of the required number of coats' [of arms].

For those right beyond the pale, who by no stretch of the imagination can lay claim to armorial bearings, shields, we are told, may be 'sentimental rather than genealogical'. They could, for instance, be charged with the emblems of virtue: such as the bee donating industry; the serpent, wisdom; the tortoise, silence; the lamb, innocence, etc. Another idea offered is to express the various professions and callings (or dare we add trades?) of ancestors and relatives by suitable emblems, if possible by treating them in accordance with the heraldic rules.

The contributor supplies us with a great deal of information about the language of heraldry into which we need not go here, but we are next invited to consider using heraldry as a decoration for the structure of the house, either externally or internally.

228 Date-tablet for the front of a house

Date-tablet

Fig 228 shows a date-tablet—a subject given much attention in earlier times. Bath or Portland stone is recommended as a suitable material, as these stones, though soft, will withstand the weather sufficiently for the purpose, and moreover, can be carved with ordinary woodcarving tools. An additional advantage is that, unlike wood, stone has no *grain* and is therefore less difficult to work upon. Here is yet one further example of the general competence in many crafts expected of readers of the magazine.

Heraldic Mantelpiece

Fig 229 shows a front elevation of the right-hand end of a mantelpiece, while Fig 230 is an end elevation of the same. This is to be carved in Caen stone or white lias. It seems to be intended to appeal to the owner of an impeccable and extensive family tree, for the tympanum over the central shield is for the crest proper to that shield, which itself would probably be made to bear arms of the owner of the house. The medallions over the shields in the jambs would also receive crests or badges while the scrolls are intended for mottoes. As a colourful addition, all the shields could be properly emblazoned.

The keen woodcarver is catered for by the heraldic enrichment of a picture frame in Fig 231 which could be used for a family portrait. The decoration is intended to be cut out in fretwork from hard wood, then carved, and fixed to the frame corners in such a way as to cover up the mitre lines.

From early times, Gothic tiles have frequently borne armorial bearings. These ideas from the past could be adapted to tiles used in fireplaces and suggested designs are given in Fig 232.

Heraldic decoration has even been applied to a capital (Fig 233), although

229 Mantelpiece with heraldic decoration   230 Section of the mantelpiece in Fig 229

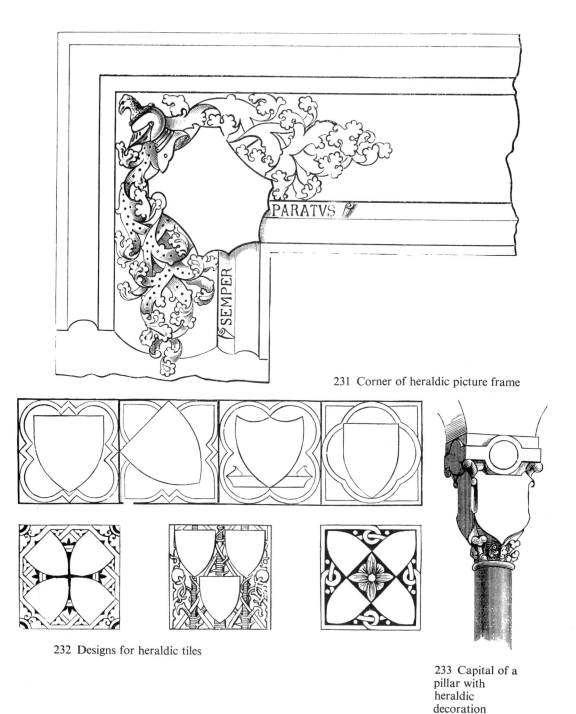

231 Corner of heraldic picture frame

232 Designs for heraldic tiles

233 Capital of a
pillar with
heraldic
decoration

the contributor has not made it clear to what use this should be put.

'It is with buildings of the Gothic and Elizabethan styles that heraldic glazing is most appropriate.' Stained glass, glass mosaic that is, shows up the full beauty and lustre of armorial designs, while with mere glass painting, in enamel colours, much is lost. Fig 234 is a design for a light in a window of the Elizabethan style incorporating the owner's initials and arms. Little technical information is given in this series of articles since the whole subject of working in stained glass is dealt with elsewhere in the magazine.

Some guidance is given on the use of heraldic designs in a kind of leather mosaic applied to the decoration of chair backs, cushions and screens. Since leather was, and is, available in a variety of colours, pieces could be cut out and fitted together (not sewn) in the manner of a stained-glass window. This craft was more successful on fairly rigid surfaces since the Victorians had not yet invented an adhesive flexible enough for use on soft, yielding and elastic foundations.

234 Window light in the Elizabethan style

Use of Cast-iron

Possibly the most ambitious application of heraldry was in the production of castings in metal—usually in iron. The magazine, generally, gives the impression that it was not difficult to find a foundry which would produce castings from patterns made by the amateur—surely this would be quite difficult today?

Fig 235 is the plate of a doorknocker intended to be cast in iron, the round boss at the bottom being the point on which the hammer strikes. The shield is 'for the arms of the master of the house' and above is his crest. The scroll on the hammer (Fig 236) is for his motto. Technical details recommend the modelling of the plate and hammer in clay, followed by the production of a mould in plaster of Paris. From this mould a cast in wax or plaster would serve as a pattern at the foundry. If this cast is of plaster, it can be saturated with boiled oil and then covered in black lead, thus giving a good surface for leaving the foundry's moulding loam and also giving the modeller a good idea of how the final product will appear. We are told that the cost of casting this knocker in iron 'is the merest trifle'!

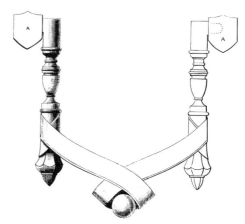

236 Hammer for the door-knocker in Fig 235: the scroll is to carry the family motto

235 Door-knocker with shield for the householder's arms

In the 1880s there was a revival of interest in cast-iron firebacks, originally the object of elaborate decoration in the seventeenth century. There is a further revival of interest today—originals fetch good prices and there is a brisk sale for good quality reproductions.

A suggested design is given in Fig 237. Considerable skill would be needed to produce a good quality model in clay, for moulding in plaster and final casting at a foundry—it is difficult to imagine many amateurs embarking on such a feat.

237 Iron back-plate for a fireplace

7
'AMUSEMENTS... OF A PHILOSOPHIC CHARACTER', TOYS, RECREATIONS AND ODDITIES

C.M.W. has for sale an alarum clock, which being set to any required time, will strike a match, ignite a lamp, boil water, make tea, coffee etc, pour out the same, and afterwards awaken the sleeper with a bell. Price 18s 6d. (1883)

Not a few novelists have given us the impression that the Victorian pater-familias was a stern figure, remote from his family, who appeared only to conduct family prayers morning and evening, and carve the Sunday joint, but was otherwise invisible for the remainder of each day.

Doll's House

But even the title of the paper on doll's-house making, 'A House for Dolly', paints another side of the picture, revealing perhaps a softer side of these be-whiskered gentlemen. The contributor of these papers wished to get away from the ordinary toy-shop concept of a doll's house—in effect a box divided into four compartments to represent rooms and carrying a plain front pierced with five windows, one at the top and bottom on either side, with another above a painted door in the middle of the front.

The usual preamble shows the kind of household for which this toy was intended, for the Editor (who wrote the articles himself) says:

> If I were a little girl, which I am not . . . I should infinitely prefer a house that would allow my having a dining-room, a drawing-room, kitchen, bedroom, day-nursery and night-nursery, to a pair of rooms, sitting-room and bedroom contained in the doll's house of ordinary mould.

He was evidently thinking of a prosperous household which possessed all these amenities in real life. And, in praising his design, the Editor remarks: 'A slight movement is all that is required to close the house, and when its owner is tired of playing with it, she, or her nurse-maid, can shut it up without trouble.'

Travelling per Kite

ONE OF THE RISING GENERATION writes: (1) I have seen pictures somewhere of people travelling by kites. Can you tell me how it is done, please? (2) Is it only possible to travel on *terra firma* or can you travel in mid-air as well? (3) What will be the probable cost of kites? To this I can only reply: (1) I have never seen pictures of people *travelling* by kites, though I know there are some people in this world who try to add to their means by *kite-flying*! I think you must be alluding to kite-flying in China and Japan, which is carried on extensively as a national sport, and have taken your ideas from pictures of this, which I have seen, I think, in *The London Illustrated News*, some years ago. If the kite were strong enough and large enough to take you off your legs, you would have to go wherever the wind carried the kite. You could exercise no controlling power over it, and you would not come down when and where you would. And consider the mess you would get into if the strings of other kites crossed yours, (2) Have you ever seen a boat or balloon? If so, you must know that it is possible to travel by water and through the air, as well as on *terra firma*. (3) It is not possible to reply to your third question. And now let me ask you *one* question in my turn. Do you not think, if you can think at all, that the exercise of a little common sense and a moderate amount of reflection would have saved you from asking, and me from answering, as far as I have done so, *three* such palpably ridiculous queries as those you have propounded above? I find a place for them for much the same reason as farmers nail hawks and magpies to a barn-door when they have shot them. . . . —Ed.

Fig 238 gives a general idea of the house, half opened on its castors. When closed, we see the frontage of a four-roomed house with two attics above. When opened, all six rooms are exposed and easily accessible for playing with.

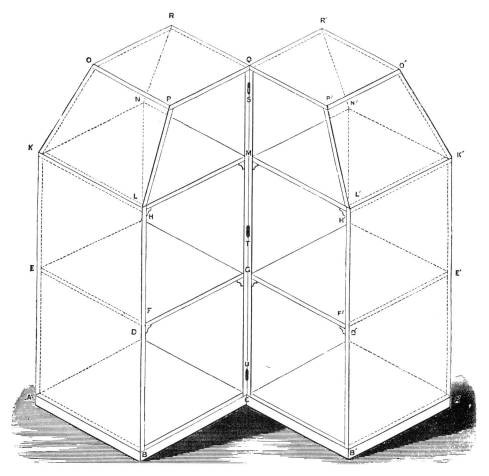

238 Doll's house: perspective view of the interior

At this point the Editor seems to forget his more wealthy readers with their day and night nurseries and nurserymaids and suggests that as the main rooms are cubic in shape, some amateurs may like to make up such a doll's house from 'a couple of boxes in which tins of lobster or salmon have been brought to this country'.

Figs 239 and 240 show the completed house—a model of a substantial Victorian detached villa complete with those embellishments designed to give an impression of some affluence. Note the chimneys, parapet and quoins, or dressings, and the treatment of the attic windows and roof. Regarding the triangular ornament between the attic windows the Editor digresses outrageously (but at the same time in a manner most interesting to the student of history).

This may be in fretwork, but carved work is, I think, preferable, and it may take advantage of a display of armorial bearings, of the family to which the little owner of the house belongs, if that family is really entitled to them. Too little respect is paid to heraldry at the present day. I should like to see

137

239 Doll's house: front view   240 Doll's house: side view

all who assume armorial bearings, without being able to prove their right
to them, charged at least treble rate of duty for the assumption; and as
trademarks very largely partake of the nature of heraldic insignia, it is only
fair and right that anyone who assumes a trademark for the better distinc-
tion of his goods should pay a tax for the use of it, as every *armiger* or
gentleman is compelled to do who openly bears his arms. I have been led
into a slight digression, which I beg respectfully to offer to Mr Childers as
an idea for the Budget of 1884—if he is then still in office.

(Mr H. C. E. Childers *did* present the Budget in 1884, but there is no evidence
that he took the advice of the Editor).

The house was intended to be really well made—not a rushed job to amuse
an impatient child: Figs 241, 242, 243 and 244 showing details of construction,
emphasise this. The 'tiles' were to be carved from strips of thin wood and the
time needed to cut out the quoins must have been considerable, but without
the benefits of 'canned' entertainment, the Victorian no doubt felt more
inclined to spend his evenings actively. The central line in Fig 239 is, of course,

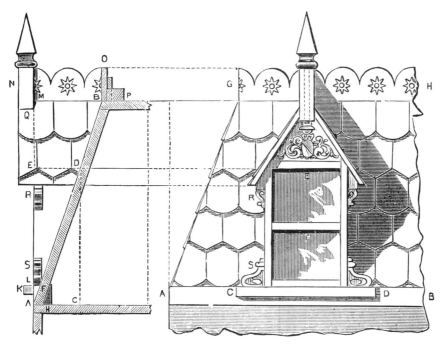

241 Doll's house: side view of attic window

242 Doll's house: front view of attic window

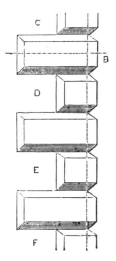

243 Doll's house: quoins at angles of the house

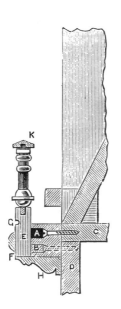

244 Doll's house: section of parapet

245 Doll's house: chimneypiece for the drawing room

the break in the front from which the house will open out to display the six rooms—this design seems an excellent idea. Except for a chimneypiece (Fig 245) the contributor has not concerned himself with the interior or its furnishings.

Moving Pictures

Before the invention of the cinematograph all kinds of scientific toys existed which depended on the phenomenon known as 'persistence of vision' to give the appearance of movement to a picture. Professor L. Marrissaux, a Frenchman who contributed several articles to *Amateur Work*, describes a number of devices to simulate motion. Fig 246, the Phenakistoscope, is one of the simplest toys to produce motion pictures. The diagram is more or less self-explanatory. On rotating the discs and looking through the slits, the figure appears to skip.

The Zoetrope, or Wheel of Life (Fig 247) which is still occasionally to be seen, is rather like a cake baking-tin mounted so as to be capable of rotation and bearing slits through which the series of pictures, drawn on a strip of paper in the lower part of the tin, are observed. Suitable strips are shown in Fig 249. The same illustrations can be used in the Praxinoscope (Fig 248) invented by M Reynaud, of Paris. This latter is a considerable improvement on the Zoetrope, for it can be operated at night, by candle light and, moreover, a group of children can surround the toy, all of them getting a good view at once. The picture seen is also brighter than in the case of the Zoetrope and the moving-picture effect is better too.

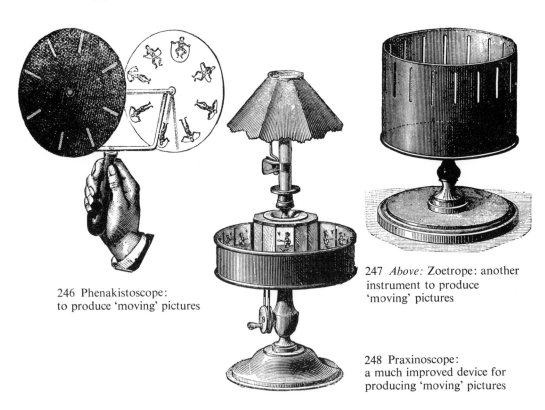

246 Phenakistoscope:
to produce 'moving' pictures

247 *Above:* Zoetrope: another
instrument to produce
'moving' pictures

248 Praxinoscope:
a much improved device for
producing 'moving' pictures

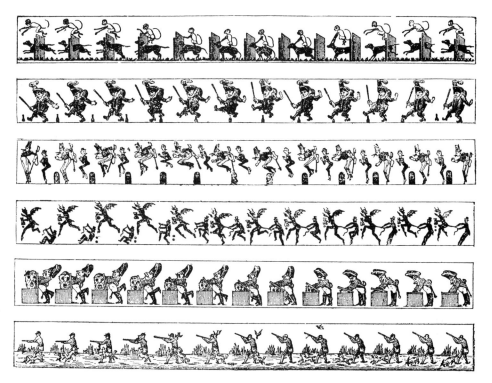

249 Pictures for the Zoetrope and Praxinoscope

... F.J.M. (*Sevenoaks*) writes: 'I have taken AMATEUR WORK from its commence-
ment ... and I have noticed the uniform kindness and courtesy with which you
have always answered correspondents. This being the case, I was surprised to
read your reply to ONE OF THE RISING GENERATION, *re* travelling per kite, and
think you should not have told him you found a place for his *palpably ridiculous
queries, for much the same reason that farmers nail hawks and magpies to barn-
doors, when they have shot them.* (The italics are F.J.M.'s, not mine.—Ed.).
After giving him such a severe talking to, you will perhaps in your next part
kindly inform him that he no doubt saw the pictures he mentioned in Vol. III
Boys' Own Paper. The first article was headed, 'Kites against Horses, or Kite-
Carriages Extraordinary, and How to Make and Use Them'. In the year 1827
there was published an extraordinary book 'Nil Mortalibus Arduum Est, The
Aeropleuristic Art; or, Navigation in the Air by the Use of Kites or Bouyant
Sails: Things unattempted yet, by George Pocock.' After many trials and
improvements in his kites, on 8th January, 1827, a carriage with six persons and
luggage did the mile in two and three-quarter minutes, and mile after mile was
completed at twenty miles per hour. Even this speed was exceeded and in 1836
Mr. Pocock of Bristol, passed through the town of Chippenham in a carriage
drawn by two kites, occasionally travelling at the rate of twenty-five miles per
hour. Running along the London Road, the carriage came up with that of the
Duke of Gloucester, who was travelling with two pairs of post-horses. The
kite-carriage passed him, drew up to let His Royal Highness go by, and then shot
past him at top speed as if he were standing still. Kite carriages were by no means
uncommon. The old Duke of Cambridge (father of the present Commander-in-
Chief) had one with silken kites, and instead of driving in the park used to go
out for an evening ride up and down the Edgware Road. ... You will I am sure,
in fairness to ONE OF THE RISING GENERATION, inform him that on pages 57, 68
and 93 of Vol. III of the *Boys' Own Paper* he will find full directions how to make
both kites and carriages!' My object in making the remarks you have italicised in
your communication was to warn others against seeking information that is

absolutely useless to readers of this Magazine. AMATEUR WORK is a practical magazine, and no room can be found in it for vain speculation on fads and subjects that are useless and generally impracticable. The successful experiments you cite by no means form an argument in favour of trying to get about the country by such a means of locomotion. 'One swallow,' you know, 'does not make summer' . . .

Your letter is written in a kindly and pleasant spirit, and I am glad to give it publicity. But I am still of the opinion that it is far better to stick to bicycles and tricycles . . .—Ed.

In the same year that Professor Marrissaux was writing (1887) a New Zealand reader of *Amateur Work* was asking how to construct a Beale's Choreutoscope. Apparently, Mr Beale lived in London and his instrument represented a real advance in the portrayal of movement in pictures for it could be used in a 'magic lantern', the moving image being projected onto a screen and viewed by many people. It incorporated the fundamental principle on which all 'moving pictures' depend, whether ciné films or television. That is, there must be presented to the human eye a succession of still pictures, rapidly one after the other, and no movement of each individual picture must be seen. Therefore in the Choreutoscope (and indeed in ciné-projectors) there is a shutter which cuts off the light at the moment one picture is being substituted for another and restores the light again as soon as the next picture is in place.

Frequently, the Choreutoscope (Fig 250) showed a skeleton dancing. A long glass slide moving in a wooden frame carried pictures of a skeleton in various positions. This moved through the 'magic lantern' in a series of jerks by means of a kind of ratchet. During each actual movement of the slide a shutter obscured the light from the lantern. In later models, photographs of a skeleton in different positions were substituted for pictures produced by hand, thus getting very near to a cinematograph picture, but the world had to wait till 1895 to see the first public film show.

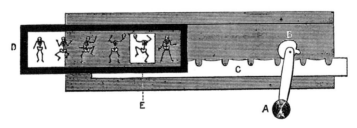

250 Choreutoscope: an instrument for showing 'moving' pictures in the 'magic lantern'

Moving Models

Entertainment by movement is taken for granted by the modern child who has grown up with cinema and television screens where the grotesque actions of his favourite cartoon characters are a never-ending source of amusement, but the Victorian child was largely denied this pleasure, as the reproduction of movement in picture form was in its infancy. Hence there was much enthusiasm for mechanical models, which possessed the added advantage that

251 Moving models: a windmill

they lent themselves to easy adaptation for the encouragement of such virtues as thrift, when serving as a money-box, or charity, when exhibited at bazaars in aid of good causes.

Fig 251 is a very simple example of a moving model—all that happens is that the sails of the windmill revolve. It is actuated by the movement of 'an eight-day timepiece' suitably modified for the purpose. The escapement is

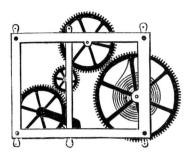

252 Moving models: clockwork adapted for the windmill in Fig 251

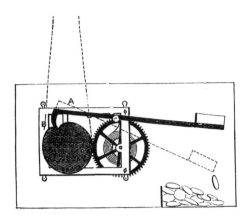

253 Moving models: a windmill—interior of the bottom of the case showing the effect of dropping in coins

removed and the hour and minute-hand mechanism united by a drop of solder at the end of the spindle of the central wheel. Fig 252 shows the adapted clock mechanism while Fig 253 indicates where a wooden pulley wheel, with a nick at one point, has been secured to the spindle which formerly carried the minute hand. The dotted lines show the string going up to the windmill to turn the sails round. Starting and stopping mechanism is provided by the arm,

254 Moving models: clockwork dancers

shown as a thick line in Fig 253, carrying a scoop for pennies at one end and a claw which falls into the nick in the wooden pulleywheel at the other. One coin will then ensure one complete revolution of the pulleywheel, but as the pulley-wheel is twelve times larger than the axle of the model mill, the sails will revolve twelve times each time it is started. We are assured by the inventor that the model will work 192 times without attention and net 16 shillings (80p) in so doing. If this were made in the present day, to work on 5p pieces, it would be a useful adjunct for the encouragement of children's savings! Two more models, actuated by clockwork, are shown in Figs 254 and 255.

255 Moving models: yacht which pitches, tosses and rolls on moving waves

In the case of the Negro minstrels, both figures are made to dance by being connected to the clockwork by an eccentric, together with a pendulum effect produced in both legs of the dancer and in the bent leg of the banjoist.

The simulation of pitching, tossing and rolling needed for the yacht calls for further adaptation of the clockwork. Fig 256 shows the clockwork supported on a cross-piece inside the case of the model and the hull of the yacht held on a lever O, pivoted to the case at N. All the connections at N, C and F are quite loose, allowing for very free movement. Figs 256 and 257, examined together,

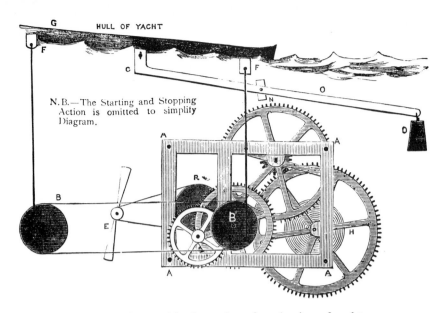

256 Moving models: front view of mechanism of yacht

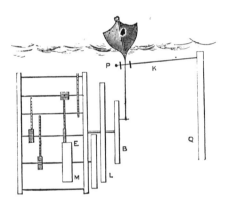

257 Moving models: side view of mechanism of yacht

show that a variety of movement is given to the boat when the clockwork is in action. The 'fly' E is a kind of fan which, offering resistance to the air, slows down the clockwork movement. A similar device is often seen in church and other large clocks. The waves are ingeniously contrived and caused to move by fastening a piece of greenish-blue silk to the hull and extending it, while quite loose, to the sides of the case. This can be touched up with white paint to show wave crests and, as the boat moves, so also do the waves.

. . . GETTING GREY ON THE TOP writes: I remember when at school in a town on the old coach road from Bristol to London, to have seen a carriage drawn by a pair of kites pass through the town. The carriage was a kind of bath-chair on two wheels, with a third guiding wheel in front; it carried two gentlemen. The kites were said to be made of silk, with very long silk cords to restrain their steady course above the town. The kites were visible long before the carriage came into view, and after it had passed out of sight. I do not remember if they had any other check on their journey, but the 'Old Bear' on his support, which crossed Hunger-ford Street, compelled them to stay and pass the lines over this barrier [an inn sign which was mounted right across the road]. As it is fifty years ago my memory does not enable me to furnish exact details, but I send these in case they are of interest to your correspondent.

Finally, the author of the original articles in the *Boys' Own Paper* writes to confirm the truth of all that has gone before:

Briefly, the statements in the *Boys' Own Paper*, in the third and sixth volumes, on the subject of Kites, Kite Carriages and Kite Boats, are facts ... Mr. Alfred Pocock, of Kingswood Hill, Bristol, one of the old kite travellers, will, I know, be glad to supply the kites to order on reasonable terms, and give particulars as to their management.

258 Moving models: waterwheel, fountain, and see-saw—all actuated by water power

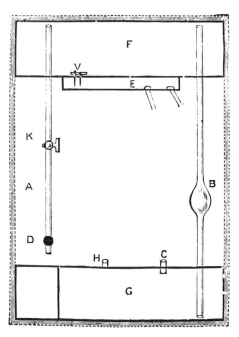

259 Moving models: pipes and tanks for the model in Fig 258

Fig 258 shows a model incorporating three moving objects, a waterwheel, a fountain and a see-saw, worked in this case by water power. A virtue claimed for the model is that real water is used in the fountain and waterwheel. Figs 259 and 260 show the principle on which it works. At the top and bottom of the case are two metal tanks and below the top tank F in Fig 259 is a smaller tank E. From E pipes lead to the trough above the waterwheel and to the fountain. C in the same sketch is connected to the pond below the fountain thus returning the fountain water to tank G. Pipe A in Fig 259 admits air to tank F when the

147

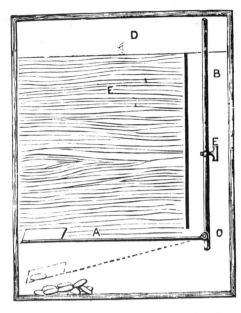

260 Moving models: side view of Fig 258 showing the starting lever

starting cock D, actuated by coins on the lever shown in Fig 260, is opened.
The rate at which air goes into tank F (Fig 259) is governed by the extent to
which the cock K is opened—a matter for adjustment when the model is set up.
(The contributor has made this slightly confusing by using different lettering
in Figs 259 and 260. V in Fig 259 is supposed to be a tap leading from tank F
to tank E.)

To get the model ready for working, suppose the tank G to be full of water.
The compress ball B (containing a non-return valve) is worked to raise the
water to tank F, the starting cock and tap K being open. The starting cock is
then closed and tap V opened. No water will escape into tank E until money
is put in to open the starting cock, when air will go up through pipe A to tank
F, allowing water to enter tank E and actuate the waterwheel and fountain.
The length of time the model works, of course, depends upon the amount of
air which has entered tank F, allowing water to escape, and this in turn is
controlled by the extent to which tap K is opened. The see-saw operates off a
spindle connected to the waterwheel.

Smoke Pictures

The making of smoke pictures (Fig 261) was also a pastime of the period. They
were produced to offer as presents to friends or as objects for sale at charity
bazaars. The materials required were very inexpensive, consisting only of
white card, a candle, needles of various sizes fixed into wooden holders, a
camel-hair brush and a penknife. The dry camel-hair brush is used to lighten
areas such as the tops of the trees and the moonlight on the water (Fig 262).
Needles of various sizes are used for lines of different thicknesses. The final
picture can be preserved behind glass.

261 Smoke picture: an example of a finished picture

262 Smoke picture: beginning the picture

Marionettes

Children, in the main, were easily entertained by a 'show'—be it a Punch and Judy show, a 'magic lantern' show or a marionette theatre. Directions are given in our magazine for a theatre of a size 'suitable for an audience of from 100 to 150 children', with 'characters' about 16in in height—the word 'puppet' is not used.

Fig 263 shows the theatre ready to use while Fig 264 shows the framework of the stage, based as it is, on a plain wooden table. The method of lighting the stage was extremely hazardous, consisting of a brass tube AB in Fig 265 closed at one end (A), and connected to the town gas-supply by rubber tubing at B. The actual illumination was obtained by lighting the gas issuing from a series of small holes drilled in the tube along its length. This must have constituted a first class fire risk (indeed, the contributor tells of his curtains catching fire on one occasion) and the illumination obtained would have been feeble. For interior scenes the writer relied largely on drapery, while outdoor scenes were painted in watercolours on white holland—a material commonly used for house-blinds at that time. The writer was sufficiently informed to realise that

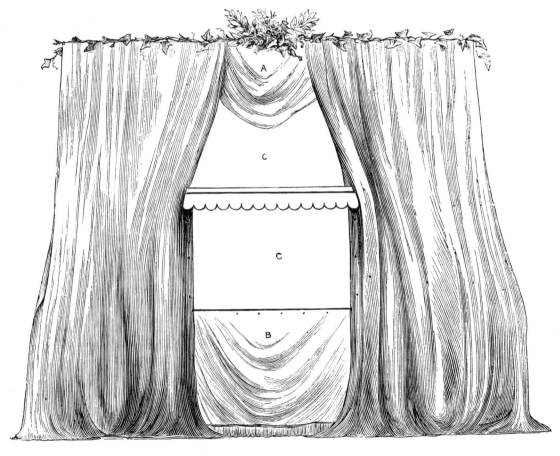

263 Marionette theatre: complete

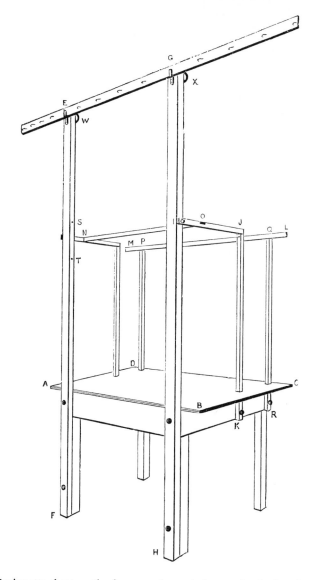

264 Marionette theatre: the framework erected on a simple, but firm, table

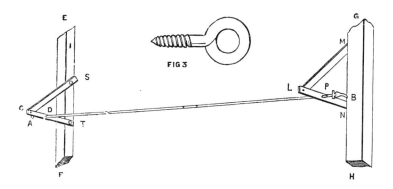

265 Marionette theatre: arrangement for gas lighting

he might produce scenery by back-projection from a 'magic lantern' but he appreciated that the puppet operators would probably get in the way of the projection beam.

For the puppets, the contributor adapted dolls' heads, the bodies being jointed in the usual way with puppets and manipulated exactly as we do today. The kind of play in favour was based upon well known fairy tales and if a fearsome dragon (Fig 266) was needed, so much the better. This creature's head was constructed from a badger's skull, and the tapering and articulating tail from a succession of chemists' chipboxes (pillboxes made from thin wood shavings), diminishing in size from body to tail tip.

Transformation scenes were popular in the real theatre and of course had to be duplicated in its toy counterpart. Lowering the gaslight for a short time made easy the substitution of Prince Charming for the Beast in 'Beauty and the Beast'. It seems that our contributor dressed and produced one play per year and hawked it round the children's gatherings in his neighbourhood.

266 Marionette theatre: dragon puppet

Conjuring

The Vanishing Lady

Conjuring was a popular entertainment, whether involving sleight-of-hand tricks which demanded much practice on the part of the performer, or the spectacular illusion, which was costly to produce, but depended more on the showmanship ability of the professor of magic and less on his powers as a conjurer. As an example of the kind of illusion thought to be within the capability of the amateur conjuror I have chosen 'The Vanishing Lady'. Invented by Buatier de Kolta (Joseph Buatier, 1845–1903) in 1886, it was shown in England in that celebrated home of magic—the theatre of Messrs Maskelyne and Cooke. As a keen spectator of *legerdemain*, I am very glad that I was able to see Jasper, Noel and Mary Maskelyne perform in their family theatre on several occasions before it was destroyed by one of Hitler's bombs in World War II.

The trick consists of sitting a lady in an ordinary chair, covering her with a large shawl or cloth 'under which her form is distinctly visible, but on removing the cloth, she has utterly vanished'. In conjuring, however, things are seldom what they appear and the chair is far from ordinary. The trick necessitates a stage trap, so is only suitable for a stage so equipped or, as we are told, the amateur conjurer in his own drawing room or village hall, can surmount this problem by causing the illusion to take place on a small stage or platform (Fig 267) in which a trap has been contrived. If this is above eye-level and the improvised stage surrounded by curtains, the trap can be used effectively.

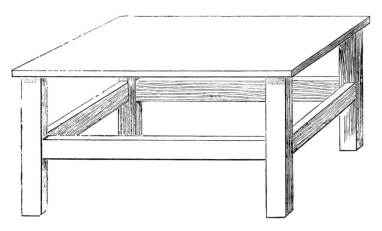

267 The Vanishing Lady Illusion: temporary stage

The essential equipment is the chair, specially constructed for this illusion. It must be substantial and a little wider at the back than the lady who is to vanish. The back (Fig 268) is covered and there is no front rail below the seat level. The frame must be solid and firm without the seat itself, A, which, together with the top rail B, is hinged along the back rail D, so that the seat can fold down as shown by the dotted line in Fig 269. In order to sit in it, the seat is kept up by two bolts (one is shown at H in Fig 269) under the frame of the chair. Hinged to the back of the chair is an iron clamp, shown raised in Fig 270 and lowered in Fig 271.

To perform the illusion, a lady sits on the chair and is immediately covered by a large shawl or cloth while the amateur showman distracts the attention of his audience with patter. On adjusting the shawl he brings the clamp up over the lady's head, so that when she has gone, the clamp seems to indicate that she is still under the shawl. The lady undoes the bolts under the seat and lowers herself through the trap while the drapery adjustments are being made, so that actually there is nobody under the shawl for most of the time the illuson is being shown. The lady closes the seat bolts again, shuts the trap and gets away under the portière curtain or other draperies. To complete the illusion, the conjurer removes the shawl with a flourish, at the same time lowering the clamp behind the chair.

The helpful contributor gives a sample of appropriate patter, a little of

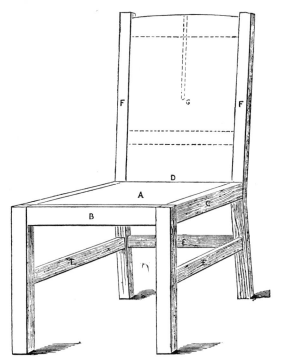

268 The Vanishing Lady Illusion: construction of the special chair

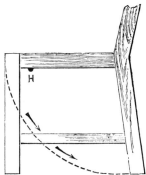

269 The Vanishing Lady Illusion: side view of the chair showing how the seat falls

270 The Vanishing Lady Illusion: iron claw which supports the shawl when the lady 'vanishes'

271 The Vanishing Lady Illusion: iron claw in position when not in use

which is reproduced below. It shows the sort of thing which a late nineteenth-century audience was likely to accept as 'a source of innocent merriment', as W. S. Gilbert had written in *The Mikado* only two years before this article appeared.

Ladies and Gentlemen—I have now the pleasure of showing you one of the newest scientific illusions of the age. The times in which we live are times of rapid progress and advancement, one discovery succeeding another with marvellous rapidity. The spread of education has rendered it necessary for even our amusements to partake of a philosophic character, and though some may be inclined to think that a conjuring trick is a poor result to be striven for, I am sure you will not say so when you know the capabilities of, and the useful purposes to which the discovery I am about to show you may be applied. Let me give you an instance: Yesterday, after my performance, a gentleman came to me and implored my assistance. Oh, dear! he looked miserable, so miserable and careworn that I pitied him from the bottom of my heart. I asked him what he wanted me to do, but instead of giving me a direct answer, he wished to know if I could vanish anybody. Of course I assured him I could, nothing easier. At last he seemed convinced, and with wonder I saw his countenance assume an aspect of calm repose—remarkable as a contrast to his haggard appearance when he came to me. Ah!, ladies, and especially gentlemen, I had given a fellow-creature back again the joy and happiness of childhood, all in a few minutes. Was not that worth doing? I myself beamed with pleasure in sympathy, and I wished I could make all mankind as happy as I had made my new acquaintance. His smile, I assure you, was perfectly angelic, and my own bosom was swelling with great and good thoughts, when he leaned towards me and breathed rather than spoke: 'Would you, oh! would you come to my house and vanish my mother-in-law?'

Heliographs

In the late nineteenth century, the telegraph, although more common than the telephone, was certainly not to be found in many parts of the undeveloped colonies, so that the heliograph still had its part to play, in the Boer War, yet to come, and on the North-West Frontier of India. Even in World War II, I was able to find two army heliographs in the armoury of the Junior Training Corps of the school where I was signals officer and we tried them out on the Surrey hills over considerable distances. Such pieces are now snapped up by collectors, largely because of their beautiful brass-work.

The correspondence columns of *Amateur Work* attracted queries on heliographs not only from a reader in Natal but also from someone in the homeland who wanted to signal across a valley three miles wide. Two answers were forthcoming. In both cases the instrument described was very simple, not possessing the accuracy of army instruments. The first example in Figs 272, 273, 274 and 275 merely consisted of a round mirror A on a flat board, supported on a stand. The mirror could be flashed by exposing it on removing a shutter

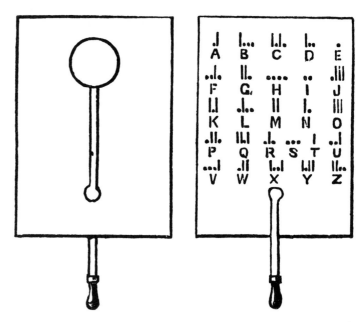

272 Heliograph: front view
of simple instrument

273 Heliograph: back view of
the instrument in Fig 272

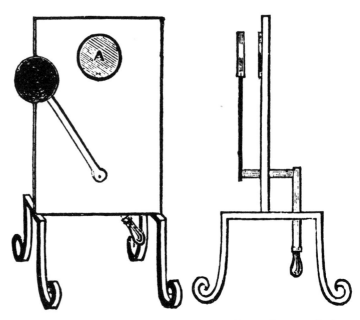

274 Heliograph: side view of
the instrument showing how
the shutter obscures the
mirror

275 Heliograph: general view
of the front

attached to a handle H. To help the beginner, the Morse code was printed on the back of the board. Although not illustrated, the amateur was told to mount a second mirror on some kind of universal joint so that the sun's rays could be directed on to the signalling mirror, irrespective of the position of the sun in the sky. This all sounds rather crude, but a later correspondent, in Natal, says he had made such a heliograph and used it over a distance of thirty miles. For shorter distances the Natal correspondent recommends an even simpler design shown in Figs 276 and 277. The dotted line in Fig 276 is an elastic band used to keep that end of the hinged board down, except when it is pressed at C to flash the mirror. Very 'Heath Robinson' methods are offered for siting one heliograph station on its counterpart away in the distance.

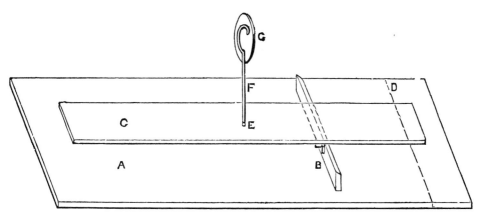

276 Heliograph: a simple form

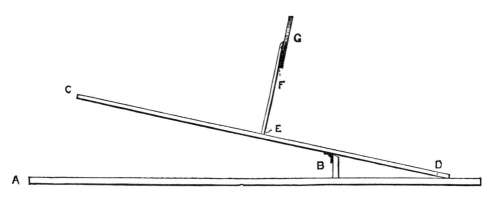

277 Heliograph: side view of Fig 276

Clothes Dryer

The folding and revolving clothes dryer now found in so many small gardens is by no means a modern invention, for in 1882 a contributor describes and illustrates such a contrivance (Fig 278) which he copied from a dryer seen by him in America. Today's versions have changed little from this early specimen.

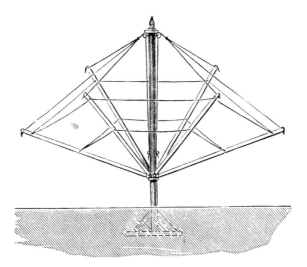

278 Clothes dryer of 1882, called an American dryer

Aids for Babies

A gentleman from Leeds inquired how to make a 'baby-jumper'—presumably similar to the present-day baby-bouncer which is controlled by springs. Sadly, he received no reply. However, his second question regarding a baby's go-cart elicited a reply from Cornwall describing how to make the contrivance shown in Fig 279 which is almost identical in general principle to our baby-walkers. The contributor says that he had heard of go-carts for teaching children to walk, but had never seen one: hence the illustration is his own invention. The diagram is self-explanatory but the comments on its mode of use deserve quotation

279 A so-called go-cart, invented in 1883, to assist a baby in its first steps

To put the child in, lift the loose piece A, put the child's feet down through the top, then replace the piece [which locks under B], stand back with an orange or some sweets, and you will find yourself repaid with the joy of the child and the praises of a loving mother, and of a relieved nurse.

Once again, it is taken for granted that the readers of the magazine have well staffed households.

Hookahs

Another gentleman from Leeds inquired how to make a hookah. As he soon received two replies, he was evidently not the only reader who wanted to smoke in this way. Fig 281 shows a simple hookah made from a pickle-jar, a large cork bung, a clay pipe of a type known as a French straw, in which the bowl is more or less in line with the stem (Fig 280), and a short piece of clay pipe joined to a rubber tube. A few drops of perfume are put in the water 'charge the pipe-head with tobacco, light, and you are in Paradise'. Figs 282 and 283 show a more elaborate hookah suggested by a Glasgow reader. It was pointed out that a hookah 'is much cleaner and less injurious than the common pipe, as the smoke is washed by passing through the water'.

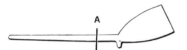

280 Hookah: a clay pipe of special shape cut off for use in making a hookah

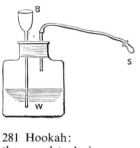

281 Hookah: the complete device

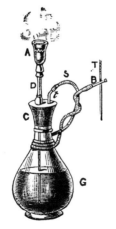

282 Hookah: a more elaborate pattern

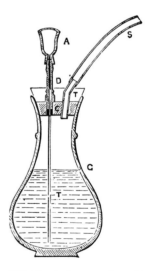

283 Hookah: a section of the hookah in Fig 282

Sleepers' Alarms

Quite a number of *Amateur Work* correspondents confess to being heavy sleepers. No particular reasons are given for this, but perhaps the lack of disturbance by traffic noise and the custom of continuing balls and dances until the early hours of the morning had something to do with it. A *cri de coeur* from one man asks:

> Is there any kind of machine (electric or otherwise) that would aid you— say, by pitching you out on the floor, pulling the clothes off you, or any other way? And if so, could you say where it is sold, and at what price?

The Editor suggests a mixture of self-resolution, pertinacity of purpose and perseverance in equal parts—a dose to be taken every morning, but a number of other correspondents sent in their methods of turning mechanical alarm clocks into electric alarms with a switching-off device outside the bedroom door, so that the victim has to get up to quell the din. The simplest, cheapest and probably the most unpleasantly effective method was submitted by Mr Shodoonkek of Sierra Leone:

> If R.H.J. should find the mixture prescribed by the editor hard to take, let him procure a large tin cup with a hole in the bottom, and suspend it over a smaller vessel to be placed directly over his head on a very narrow shelf or piece of board projecting over the head of his bed. The larger vessel is to be then filled with water which will pass through the hole at the bottom in drops to fill the vessel beneath it. As soon as this small vessel is filled, the water will trickle over the sides to the face or head of the sleeper, who not liking such a nice good morning will hasten out of bed. The size of hole in the bottom of the vessel . . . must be determined by experiment.

In spite of his fear of things 'frivolous or inappropriate', the Editor makes no unfavourable comment on this.

Electric Lamp Lighter

Electric light for domestic use still being rare, 'An Electric Lamplighter' appearing in 1888, is the title of a paper describing how an electric device can cause a match to be struck and applied to a benzoline lamp, which, on being lit up, awoke a sleeper who was insensitive to alarms depending on noise, but who reacted immediately when a light was struck. (Benzoline is a mixture of low-boiling-point paraffins.)

The complete instrument is shown in Fig 284 where the end of an ordinary safetymatch is seen in a holder, attached to the top shelf. (This is shown more clearly in Fig 285.) The coiled spring in Fig 285 would normally keep the matchholder pointing outwards from the instrument, as indicated by the dotted line in the plan view (Fig 286), but it is kept parallel to the back board by a spring when the device is set. The curved support on the left of Fig 286 carries a piece of the prepared striking surface from a matchbox, so that when the

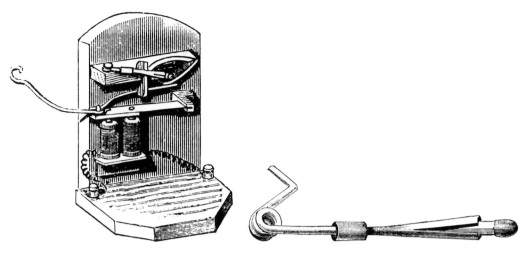

284 Electric lamp lighter: front view   285 Electric lamp lighter: the matchholder

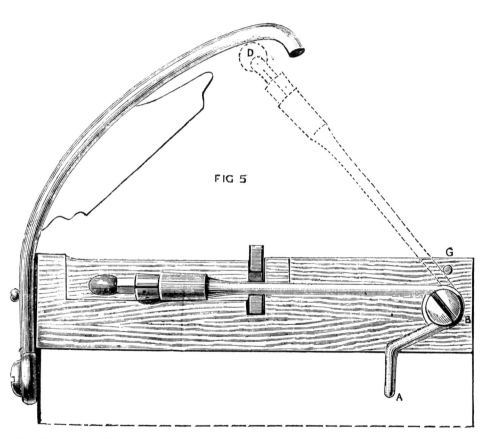

FIG 5

286 Electric lamp lighter: plan of the device showing the match striking the prepared surface (from a matchbox)

matchholder is released the matchhead rubs against the striking surface and ignites the wick of the benzoline lamp, indicated by the dotted circle D in Fig 286. The trigger holding the match is released by the electromagnet seen at the base of Fig 284, this electromagnet being connected into the circuit of an electric-bell alarm clock in such a way that the current must pass through the electromagnet in order to actuate the alarm. It all sounds very uncertain in its action, but the contributor assures us that it was most effective and even adds suggestions for its adaptation for lighting a coalgas jet in place of an oil lamp (but he does not tell us how the gas was turned on at the right moment).

Making Use of Odds and Ends

Among many bright ideas for the use of superfluous objects are suggestions for using a large quantity of empty cotton reels. The reader who raised the question thought of making them into a summerhouse. (Although he gives no clue as to how he meant to do this, I think he intended threading them on rods to form a kind of trellis.) He got a very abrupt reply from one reader— burn them in the grate! Another man, however, supplied this sketch (Fig 287) showing how they could be used as a substitute for turned legs when making up occasional tables, whatnots, etc.

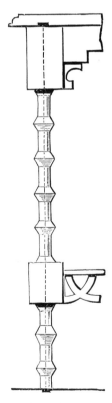

287 Use for cotton reels:
a table leg made from
empty reels

288 Uses for tin cans: birds' nests

289 Uses for tin cans:
a gluepot

290 Uses for tin cans:
bread grater

291 Uses for tin cans:
fruit gatherer

Amateur Work frequently reminds us how the reader can economise by making things for himself. On the principle of 'waste not, want not', a contributor indicates many uses for old tin cans—the illustrations once again giving us a picture of living conditions among the middle classes ninety years ago. Fig 288 shows a tree rather reminiscent of a crowded modern housing estate but showing various designs for 'bird houses'. Weather-proofing was achieved by dipping the cans in molten asphalt, afterwards rolling them in sand, dry packing-moss (used by florists), short dry twigs, or even small fircones.

Of greater utilitarian value are the gluepot (Fig 289) and breadcrumb-maker (Fig 290), while from personal trial I can recommend the fruit-gatherer (Fig 291) in which the rim of the tin is filed to a sharp edge and the inside lined with a cloth bag to receive the fallen fruit without bruising.

The hanging log (Fig 292) is made from a tin can, first asphalted and then surrounded by birch bark. A hanging flowerpot (Fig 293) is made up on similar lines and decorated with small cones, burrs or acorns. Fig 294 is described as an ornamental vase for dried grasses and autumn leaves and was contrived from 'a broken lamp standard of glass' surmounted by a tin can dipped once again in asphalt and embellished with selected lichens, shells and parts of pinecones. I have a feeling that modern flower arrangers would copy Queen Victoria in exclaiming, 'We are not amused'.

292 Uses for tin cans: hanging log decoration

293 Uses for tin cans: hanging flowerpot

294 Uses for tin cans: ornamental vase

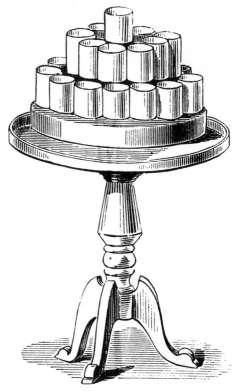

295 Uses for tin cans: arrangement of cans for a plant stand

296 *Left:* Uses for tin cans: plant stand complete

Fig 295 shows the initial stage in the construction of the contributor's *pièce de résistance*—a plant stand as a centrepiece for a bay window (Fig 296). The materials needed for this ornament all date from a bygone age, for, having procured an old occasional table, two cheeseboxes were next needed, one larger than the other. These were circular containers made of very thin wood, placed one above the other on the table. To prevent tin cans falling off the table, wooden hooping from a flour barrel was nailed round the rim. On the cheeseboxes tin cans were arranged in the manner shown. The cheeseboxes were secured in place by putty, and the cans, cheeseboxes and table-top all made watertight with asphalt. One hole bored in the table-top afforded an escape for surplus water. Inevitably, the tin cans were ornamented with burrs, cones, lichens or treebark. The open space between the first circle of pots and the table was filled with earth, on top of which moss was built up to the first circle of tin cans. Gardeners will note with interest that the plants recommended for the tin cans are *Tradescantia*, common and variegated ivy, periwinkles, saxifrages, hyacinths, stonecrops, ferns and the calla lily.

297 Barrow for tumblers on a dining-table

298 Barrow to hold a covered dish

166

One of the many clerical contributors tells us how to make the little barrows in Figs 297 and 298. He says he has made many of these as presents for friends and also for sale at his church bazaar. They were made of deal off-cuts, the wood being left in its natural colour. We are told that they were also suitable for carrying breakfast cruets, jam jars and potted meats.

Gun-wads

Surely the prize for originality of ideas in using unwanted materials must go to the gentleman from Aldershot (appropriately enough) who devised a decorative use for gun-wads. To the uninitiated, it should perhaps be explained that at one time it was common for sportsmen to fill their own cartridges, and to do so the materials were kept in place in the paper cartridge by discs of cardboard. The contributor says he had many spare gun-wads since he had recently taken to buying filled cartridges. He tells us that he made a number of shelf brackets but felt that their general appearance was rather stiff and angular, being in want of curved lines in their design. He did not possess a lathe, so could not turn up little balustrades, etc. Therefore, using his cut-throat razor, he bisected his circular gun-wads and, after coating them with gold paint, applied them in the manner shown (Figs 299 and 300) to his black-and-gold brackets.

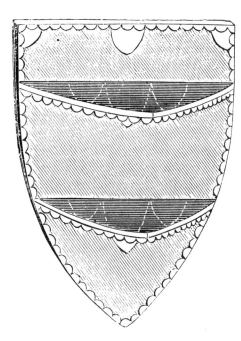

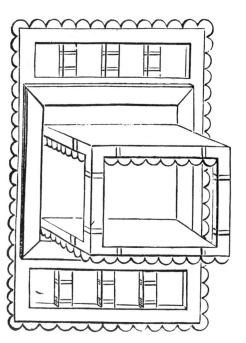

299 Use for gun-wads: ornamental bracket   300 Use for gun-wads: more elaborate ornamentation of a bracket

ACKNOWLEDGEMENTS

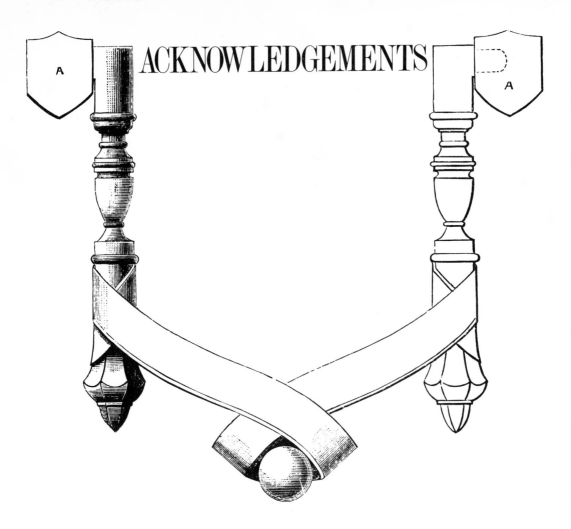

I am most grateful to L. M. Harrod, formerly Director, The National Library, Singapore, and a friend of forty years' standing, for his help, freely given, in locating valuable references; to Richard Baker, radio and television broadcaster, for permission to quote from one of his programmes; to the staff of the City of Cambridge Reference Library for most courteous attention to all my wants on every occasion and to my sister for typing the manuscript most promptly.